Restaurant Owners Uncorked part II

WIL BRAWLEY

Member of the Schedulefly Crew

ISBN: 1523730129
ISBN-13:9781523730124

"Pizza is pizza. You can have a better quality pizza, but that can always be duplicated. Someone can copy the way we make pizzas or somebody can copy the way we make pasta. People can copy the way we decorate or the music we play. The thing that's hard to duplicate is ***how you make people feel***." - Paul Wise, Christianos Pizza

CONTENTS

INTRODUCTION

This is the second book in our Restaurant Owners Uncorked series. We are fortunate at Schedulefly that over 6,500 independent restaurants are our customers because it gives us access to so many amazing restaurant owners, and we love telling as many of their stories as we can.

Twenty-one of them are featured in this book. All of them are very busy people, and were kind to offer their time to speak with us. They are not celebrity chefs and famous people. They are everyday owners who have built successful businesses and were willing to share their stories, their passion for the restaurant business, and lessons they've learned over the years.

This book is here to educate you, entertain you and inspire you. We hope you enjoy it. And we hope you start your own restaurant one day, and that you're very successful, and that when you are you will share your story with us.

Comida

RESTAURANT OWNER SINCE 1999

How did you get started in the restaurant business?

I started Proto's Pizza with my partner at the time, Pam Proto. We opened five Proto's Pizzerias together. We started with one in Longmont, CO in 1999 and opened four along the Front Range and one up in Boise, Idaho, just to try our hand out-of-state. We did that in seven years. And then I sold my half to her in 2007. After I left she opened one more and they're still going strong.

Opening five locations in seven years sounds like it was a pretty busy time.

It was pretty busy for sure. We were just scared to death for the first little bit. I think each time we opened a new location, I would just wonder how in the heck we were going to get it all done and where was the money going to come from and how to make it all happen.

But Pam is very tenacious and I learned so much from her over the years about *putting your right foot forward and showing up and working hard*. We hired really great people because obviously you can't run five restaurants alone, especially with one in an out-of-state area. It was a great opportunity. We worked really well together for that whole time.

What made you decide to branch out?

I love pizza and I love Proto's and I still eat it about once a week, but I just was sort of antsy to do my own thing.

I put myself through pastry school just before she bought me out, just to learn a part of the restaurant world that I was completely unfamiliar with and also very uncomfortable with. I didn't want to go through sixty thousand dollars' worth of chef's school, but I wanted to learn a little of the back-of-the-house side of things. So, I did the pastry thing and that was a great eye-opener for me just in terms of knowing that I never wanted to be a pastry chef. But, I still love making pastries. I just made fresh peach ice cream this morning here at home before I went to work. I love the pastry side of things from a home perspective, but not from a real-world restaurant perspective.

After that I actually bought into a small restaurant in Boulder and co-owned that for a year with someone. That restaurant is still there, but it just wasn't the right fit for me. It was an incredible learning experience on many levels, but it wasn't my lifelong "oh-this-is-going-to-be-a-great-business-

3

partnership." It wasn't exactly what I wanted to do. After a year, I worked on sort of dissolving that partnership and relationship from a business perspective.

That lead to your food truck, right?

Yes. I was ready to really do something at that point just one hundred percent on my own. I didn't have a ton of money left in terms of some extra cash in the bank to start a whole new business. I thought about what I could do on a smaller budget with a little bit less commitment perhaps than a restaurant. The food truck thing had just really started coming around. This was 2009. And in 2010 I eventually started it.

Well, it turned out *food trucks weren't legal in Boulder at the time*. I didn't know that. I didn't know only because there were none. It seemed like such a great idea to me. It didn't even cross my mind that they wouldn't be legal. I knew of somebody else that had tried to start one but it ended up not happening and I didn't know why it had failed.

I put down sixty grand on a truck in East Brunswick, NJ, was having it built out, having it shipped out on a flatbed to get to me here in Boulder. I was going through that process in trying to get city licenses and that's when I learned they were not legal, after having spent all of that money. I don't always do things in the right order (laughs). It was going to be really difficult to make it happen. Five-and-a-half years later and it's more than happening, which took a lot of hard work, especially in that first year-and-a-half.

We were trying to figure out how to not get arrested, and where can we go make money without being tracked down. Where can we go without somebody calling the cops, because I was making them mad for parking somewhere on the street, even if it was a long distance away from the front door of their restaurants? So, I didn't do that very much. I figured out another way to make money and pay the bills and when the opportunity presented itself to open a restaurant – that's when I thought this may really work. After just a year-and-a-half of running the food truck, I realized that was a hard way to make a living. The hardest, actually.

How did you build a following?

We had a lot of friends to spread the word. And Facebook was six or seven years old. As far as using it from a business platform and building my business, I would have been nowhere without that as a way to communicate with people as to how and where we were going to be once they found out about us. Having been in the restaurant business in this town for a long time, people knew what I was doing and were excited about it. And I think once they tasted it and realized it might worth driving out to a random industrial park to stand in a parking lot in line, sometimes in the snow, to get tacos. They cared. They kept coming back and they kept searching for us. But, it was not nearly as glamorous as what happened on the movie "Chef," where they just seamlessly sort of rolled across the country, stopping wherever they wanted, going to the grocery store, grabbing food and making it and then having a line. *That's not reality*.

I read an article where you said that every time you've ever second-guessed yourself it's been done out of fear, but when you jump in with both feet and do something anyway the doors kind of opened for you. How have you learned to embrace fear?

Fear is a natural part of life. It's easy to look on any number of different blogs where they talk about restaurant openings and closings within the last month, and you see how many, with very good intentions and sometimes great ideas, start and within a year they're closed. With Proto's, when we opened our doors at that first location, we had, I think, two thousand dollars in the bank account on the day that we opened. There was no room for error. There was no room at all. We had signed a lease for a long period of time, and then there we were, two of us about to make a living from one pizzeria and two thousand dollars in the bank. I think we were very lucky. Often people have the best intentions and the worst ideas.

I was actually thinking about our concept last night. People open small little sort of street side cafes but they have six tables and a small menu and they think, "I can do this. I can make this work." That's a lot like opening a food truck. You're thinking to yourself that it's a small commitment. But the bottom line is unless you show up every single day and make it work and make the food delicious and serve it in a way that makes people want to come back, they're not going to. If you only have six tables, or you just have a food truck, and a two-hour window of time during the day to feed people, if you screw that up, what do you do? With the food truck, there were times when we would spend three hours prepping in the morning. We'd go out and it would be a bomb — we'd sell seventy dollars. With me and two other people on the truck, seventy dollars doesn't even pay for gas, let alone all of the other things.

The fear is real. And you have to manage it and also manage all of the moving parts that make up service in the service industry in regards to

5

restaurants. It's a lot. And a lot of people don't know what they're doing. A lot of times it's naiveté. They think it looks really fun. But the bottom line is, in the middle of the night when you wake up at two-thirty in the morning, you bolt up out of bed because you think to yourself, "Holy crap, it's payroll taxes, it's Wednesday tomorrow. And there's not enough money in the bank account."

What has been critical to your success?

I think having a great idea is obviously the first big thing. And then executing it well with great people who have your back is another huge piece to it. I know that good people are hard find, but I think that *good people like great management*. Often people either micromanage or they're completely hands off and then the lunatics are running the asylum, so to speak. Neither of those is a great way to manage or lead. I don't know that I do it very well on a day-to-day basis, but I think I must do a decent enough job because I really have incredible people working with me.

Have you changed your management style over the years?

Absolutely. I've had experiences with people that are total hotheads and that's clear to me that that's no way to manage or lead. Nobody likes it when people blow up at them. Leading by instilling fear in people is a great way to make people not want to stick around. And then the opposite side of that is just being completely dispassionate and not available for people, not listening. Not watching from the extreme end of market trends to just the minutiae of what's actually happening in the dish pit today. It's a broad spectrum of stuff to pay attention to and there's only twenty-four hours in a day and some of those you have to sleep and also have a life.

This has been one of the key things for me. I'm not an hour-counter. I don't talk to people about how much I work. I don't calculate that stuff in my head unless it's been too long since I've had a day off. But in general, I feel like a good manager-owner. I have to have time for myself. It's how I regroup and show up ready to be in charge again, be the boss. *Nobody wants a boss that's just downtrodden and tired and like a martyr*. That's just a bummer to me. I wouldn't want a boss like that and I don't want anybody on my management team to be that way.

One of the questions that I ask people when I hire them, especially when they're going to be in leadership positions, is what do you like to do when you're not at work? What's important to you? Do they hike? Do they just go out to the bars all night long? Are they the kind of people that love to

6

go out and eat and enjoy the dining experience? What do they do? Do they like to read? Do they read cookbooks? Are they informed? What makes them tick? Interesting people make for interesting managers. And boring people get bored, I guess (laughs).

You got the truck in 2010, opened one location in 2012 and a second in 2013. That's intense.

It was a lot. The second restaurant, that whole opening was a crazy month's period of time. I had sold my house in order to get money to go towards the opening of the new restaurant and just timing all of that and getting a loan and the SBA, the bank and all of that stuff. Thank God I have an amazing bookkeeper who works for me pretty much full time and she has really neat handwriting and is a great bean-counter. Those are the little things and sometimes my time is better spent doing other things.

Two weeks after opening the first Comida location I moved into a new house. The day I moved in was the day the 100-year flood came to Boulder. It was INSANE! I grew up wanting to be an actress and wanting to be in the theater and there was always that thing — the show must go on — and that's the same thing that happens in my industry now. You still open your doors. You still show up and make food and serve it.

Are you going to keep expanding?

Yeah! Just yesterday I brought home a Sprinter cargo van. I'm growing the indoor catering piece to my business, which is really exciting. And I'm also about a week away, maybe not even that much, from signing a lease on a new location in Aurora in a building called The Stanley Marketplace. That's another incredible opportunity. It'll be the third Comida Cantina. I'm proud of the brand, I'm proud of the food. It's all made from scratch. It's not brain surgery. *It just takes showing up and doing*. And so, I'm excited to do it again. I think it'll be great.

Just showing up and doing...

Yeah, I think a lot of people might look at it as sort of plodding. "Ugh! I've got to get up again and do the same thing over again." But I am one hundred percent a morning person. I don't know how people do it without being a morning person, although my restaurants don't stay open until midnight or one o'clock, so maybe that's part of it.

I'm excited every day that I wake up and there are new challenges. And sometimes they hit you in the face like a ton of bricks. Three weeks ago, one of my very dearest, sweetest employees — she was just everything, longest tenure at Comida — very unexpectedly let me know that she needed to move on. She needed to take a job that was closer to where she lives, closer to her husband and family. It was a really hard decision for her, and it completely blindsided me. There are moments like that where you think "Holy you-know-what — how do I do this without her? What do I do? What's the next day going to be like? Who will fill her position?" But I know myself well enough to know that freaking out helps nothing. So, if I'm going to freak out I do it by myself in my car — which I did.

Then, after a good night's sleep and a bunch of just writing stuff down, different ideas, I woke up in the morning with a clear head and some ideas and had a good conversation with her, and I was okay. Within hours this amazing person who I've worked in a different sense — she's done all my graphics stuff for the last fifteen years (even since Proto's) — stepped up and said, "I'm really interested in talking to you about that position." I couldn't be luckier to have her.

If it were easy, then everybody would do it. That's one of my favorite things to say because it's true. It's just not easy. But there was the solution. I think so many people sit and spin in the problem and they show up and they talk about the problem. I had a really great boss at one point (my favorite boss, ever, really the only boss I ever had*) who said, "Rayme, if you show up to work consistently and you're thinking to yourself, I can't stand that person, why are they doing that? The only person you have to blame is yourself. You're Rayme Rossello: In charge. This is your world, your reality."

Parting thoughts?

You can either make it great or it can just suck and you can plod through it every day and that's not how I want to live or run restaurants.

* Rayme's boss was Dave Query of Big F Restaurant Group in Boulder, CO. Dave is featured in the first Restaurant Owners Uncorked book.

The Indigo Road Hospitality & Consultation

FOURTEEN LOCATIONS ACROSS ELEVEN CONCEPTS
- CHARLESTON, COLUMBIA AND FLORENCE, SC,
ATLANTA, GA AND CHARLOTTE, NC

RESTAURANT OWNER SINCE 2009

Tell me how you got into the restaurant business.

I started washing dishes at thirteen years old. I think that was illegal at the time, to be honest. They paid me three dollars an hour cash, under the table. I was at a Chinese restaurant and I was the only American in there. I had no idea what they were saying every week. But then I quickly got into cooking. I grew up in Atlanta and I opened the first Fudddruckers in Atlanta. I was sixteen and a grill cook. Then I worked the first Houston's that ever opened. After a few burns and scars, I could see through the smoke that all the pretty girls were out front (laughs). I figured out that I needed to get out there and wait tables, and that this angry chef screaming at me was not the road I wanted to go down.

I've been very fortunate. I ended up in Charleston in 1990. I was twenty-one years old and I opened Magnolia's. I met my first mentor, a guy by the name of Chris Goss, who was the visionary behind Magnolia's. That was the first time that I had somebody take me under their wing and say, "You know, Steve, people don't go out to eat to eat food. They go out to eat to *have an experience*, and we're here to create that experience." That was a light bulb moment for me. It was the first time I saw dining as something more than just the mechanics of serving somebody a plate of food. I immediately fell in love. At that point, there was no Food Network, there were no *Top Chefs*. The restaurant business was still considered what you did until you figured out what you were going to do. Everybody was always saying, "I'm just doing this until I get a real job." It always felt like a real job to me. I was working seventy or eighty hours a week and loving every minute of it.

Then I sort of fell in love with wine. I fell in love with every aspect of it. The craft cocktail thing had not happened and craft beers had not yet happened. Wine was really the thing that you learned about. From there, I opened Blossom Café in '92. Since then I've opened thirty-five restaurants and nine hotels. I've just always loved the idea that we were there to take care of people. I've never lost that enthusiasm for creating a moment for somebody that they would remember.

What goes into creating a great experience.

We talk about the experience all the time. Sometimes it's tangible and a guest will leave the restaurant and go, "God, that waiter was just amazing. They just knew the menu and they seemed so excited." As the ambassador, if you will, of the restaurant, we put a lot of energy into our service staff about creating that experience. But sometimes it's intangible. Sometimes it's just a feeling you have. I think people have varying degrees of how much they pay attention to the details. Some people will say, "God, how did they cook that rack of lamb?" For other people, going out to dinner is a social experiment. Oftentimes, it's a business dinner. Sometimes it's a first date. Sometimes it's old friends who have gotten together. There are so many different scenarios that bring people to the restaurant. And we talk about that all the time. What kind of experience is that particular table looking for? Businessmen are probably looking for efficiency and to be seen and not heard. There are so many different experiences. But, I think it kind of breaks down into tangible experiences, where people go, "That was the best pasta I've ever had in my life." Or the intangible, like, "God, what a great evening. It just felt good in there."

That comes from the people that work inside the four walls. We say this all the time. I think we build good-looking restaurants, but it's people that make a restaurant. It's our responsibility first to create and then to nurture staff that want to create that experience for guests. You can have the coolest restaurant in the world, but if you've got a server with a bad attitude waiting on you, you're not going to overcome that. The one that really gets me is when you get a server that's indifferent and you can tell that they're just going through the motions. "Hi, how are you tonight? Do you have any questions? Okay." And the food comes and maybe it's even technically correct. The food comes at an appropriate time, it tastes good, the bill comes. But you just kind of go, "Eh, well, it was pretty good." It's that intangible. There was just was nothing memorable about it. Then there's the server that says, "Hey, have you dined with us before? Thank you so much for being here. Let me tell you a little bit about our menu." You just have this feeling that "Wow, this person is really engaged in our experience."

The same goes for cooks. They may not interact directly with the guest, but we have a saying that **happy cooks cook happy food**. If we don't have a spirit of hospitality in the kitchen, then I think ultimately the food's not going to taste as good. So, we spend a lot of energy with our chefs.

We don't have the old school. What I grew up with was the yeller-screamer chefs. That's just not a culture that we allow. We talk about our priorities and the number one priority in our restaurant, believe it or not, is not the guests. The number one priority in the restaurant is the employees. Because if the employees aren't hospitable, if they're not coming to work in a positive environment, if they're not feeling inspired every day, then what kind of experience are they going to give the guest? They're going to give the guest an okay experience.

I get stopped by people that will say, "Of all your restaurants, Indaco is my favorite." But they don't really say, "Because I think the food's the best" or, "Because the service is the best." They don't know why it's their favorite — they just know it is their favorite. Oftentimes, they'll say it just feels good in there. And that has to do with the people, ultimately.

So, a great guest experience is the simply the by-product of you focusing on employees?

Yes. A guest is going to naturally have a better experience by somebody that is enjoying their job. We have to hire that, by the way. We do manager retreats three or four times a year. I get everybody in the room. We've gone from one to thirteen restaurants in seven and a half years, so it's been a rapid growth. There are decisions to be made about ways of doing things. I'm very collaborative in nature. Whenever I think we need to refine how we're doing things, I get everybody in a room and I let them be a part of the discussion. We've identified qualities, emotional qualities, that somebody really needed to have to work with us, that had nothing to do with what their resume said. We talk about the technical and the emotional. I can teach you how to ring a check up. I can teach you how to clock in. I can teach you how to put the right silverware in the right place. But I can't teach you to *genuinely care about the guest experience*. We figured out that if people are our secret sauce, if you will, then we need to be sure we're hiring the same kind of person. We're not perfect. We get it wrong sometimes. We're in an era where the labor market in the restaurant is terribly anemic. There's a lot of talk in the industry about living wages for the kitchen and work conditions and all of those sorts of things. So, we feel all that more compelled to have an environment that people want to come to. Because the truth is today, especially in a city like Charleston where there's restaurants on every corner, if a server's not happy they can walk out the door and within two hours they're going to be hired somewhere else. It really is incumbent upon us to do it right, and create an environment where people love coming to work, so our guests are just naturally going to get a better experience.

Do you think if you're doing it right then the people that leave were probably not the right fit in the first place?

Yes. I would say ninety percent of the people that leave us, whether they choose to leave us or we choose to part ways, they didn't have those emotional qualities that I mentioned. And this is true of executive chefs and general managers too. It's usually not because the server just can't seem to ring the orders in right. It's usually because they're not a team player, or in the kitchen the way they're speaking to people is just not okay. I would almost say a hundred percent of the time we've let somebody go in a senior leadership position is because their internal hospitality is not where it needs to be.

It's incredibly hard to find great people. At The Macintosh, the chef has been nominated five times for Best Chef Southeast James Beard. We were nominated by the James Beard Foundation "Best New Restaurant" in 2011. That is a restaurant that five to ten years ago would have had servers with a minimum of five years' experience. They would have had a vast knowledge of wine. Well, we just don't have that. We're not seeing those resumes anymore. So, we're having to hire to the emotional qualities and just accepting that we're going to have to spend more time training them. But if they're the right person, they're going to get it. It requires more work as a restaurant owner. But, it's the new world order. Our steakhouse, Oak, is eleven years old. We've got those older servers who know the wines. But in all of our other restaurants, we're hiring twenty-one to twenty-five-year-old people, and they don't have a ton of experience. We just have to accept that if they're the right person, though, they're going to respond to our environment. They're going to go, "Man, I love this."

I do an orientation for new hires. Anybody that's been hired within two months comes and sits. It's really very informal, but we just talk about our culture. The best thing I can hear is when somebody's been working two or three weeks at one of our restaurants and they say, "Man, I've never worked in a restaurant like this. I just love it so much." Or if somebody has been there a week I'll say, "Well, why did you want to work at O-Ku or Indaco?" and they say, "I just always heard that your restaurants are a great place to work." That's the ultimate compliment for me.

It is incredibly hard to find and keep people. I worked for Ritz-Carlton Hotels a long time ago, and I heard something in a manager training program that said that *people don't leave jobs, they leave managers*. I have found that to be universally true. In our case, there might be another restaurant down the street where the tipped employees can make more money, but if the environment's right, that's what they'll stay for. There might be five percent of the people that say, "Hey, I love working here, but I need to make more money somewhere else." But the vast majority of people quit because they're unhappy with their manager.

Are your staff members looking at your restaurant group as a long-term opportunity, since you are growing so fast, which gives them opportunities to grow their career as well?

I think so. I tell our servers, or whoever's sitting in that meeting, "Listen, if this is the career for you, if you have a lightbulb moment, maybe you walked in the door because you didn't know what else to do, maybe you quit. But if the light bulb comes on for you, you don't ever need to work with any other group again, because we have different cuisines, we're always growing, there's always an opportunity to be promoted." We're making people partners that were waiters five years ago. Kimball Brands, our managing partner for all three of the O-kus, was a waiter at Oak Steakhouse and then he became the GM at O-ku in Charleston and he just really made the restaurant what it was. So we said, "You know what? We want to do more of these and we want you to be a part of it." Jeremiah Bacon came in as a partner at Oak. We opened The Macintosh and I said, "I'm going to split every dollar I make with you." We have to do it right. We have to be all of the things that I say we are. We have to live up to our own expectations and the employees' expectations. We've had two or three people in the last year leave that we just hated to see leave. They've all come back. *That's environment, that's not compensation.* That's a hundred percent environment.

What happens when somebody you've influenced wants to start their own restaurant?

Some of our superstars want to own their own business. I've told them all I'll be there on opening night cheering them on. That's what people did for me, and I feel a responsibility to do that for the next generation. We talk a lot about mentoring the next generation. There's so much talk about the millennials and the lack of work ethic, and I'm not going to say that we haven't found that to be true at times. But, if I can take somebody who's in that age group who doesn't really know how wonderful this industry could be and turn that bulb on for them, and then they go on someday to open their own restaurant, well I've got a half a dozen names that did it for me over the last twenty years. It's kind of like I'm paying it forward.

Am I right that if some of the Millennials aren't inclined to work very hard, the ones that do have a significant career advantage?

Some of my managers are in their forties, and at times they've kind of struggled with the Millennials — struggled to connect. What I keep saying is, "Listen, guys, they are the workforce." It's that old saying "adapt or die." I see other restaurant owners and they don't feel the way I feel. There's this constant sort of "God, they suck." I keep saying, "Find the one who is willing to work hard. Let's create a life for them and try and build some loyalty with them." What I have found is when that generation feels like they have a voice, which is why I believe in collaborative environments, and when they're valued then they really prosper. Now, some of them have unrealistic expectations and having a voice doesn't mean that you always get to give them everything they want. Sometimes that gets a little confusing when we say, "Hey, we want to hear from you but we can't do everything you want us to do."

We have a twenty-six-year-old general manager at O-ku in Charleston. He'll tell you, "I grew up spoiled. I didn't know what work ethic was." He's had his moments. There have been some moments where we've had to sit him down and go, "Listen, this is the real world. I'm sorry that you're working fifty-five to sixty hours a week. I don't know what to say." I just keep trying to find ways to connect and keep communicating a message of, "Listen, there is a career here for you. But, we've got to have a mutually beneficial relationship. It can't be one-sided. It can't be all about what you want and what you need. The business has needs too."

We will spend the next decade navigating that with these folks. But, again, they are the workforce. They're not going anywhere. And the restaurant business is hard. I have worked nights, weekends and holidays for the better part of thirty years. I wouldn't have it any other way, but it's a real tricky time for our business. More restaurants than ever before are opening. But if you look nationally, attendance at culinary schools is flat. The statistics are not in our favor, which is all the more reason why we have to create an environment that people want to stay in.

What are the pros and cons of being in such a competitive market like Charleston?

It's forcing us to think more creatively. I'm paying a lot of attention to the twenty-eight to thirty year olds that are opening their own restaurants. I looked at Jeremiah Bacon, who's our chef-partner in two restaurants and is my age, and said, "Listen, in two or three years we're not the ones that need to be coming up with the creative ideas. We're just not. We need to be listening to the generation behind us." I'm paying a lot of attention to the young kids that are opening restaurants much earlier than my generation. I was forty before I was a partner in my first restaurant. Now they're working two, three, four years in a restaurant and then opening their own. I'm watching them both for what I want to learn and for what I don't want to do, because the servant-heart mentality isn't there as much anymore. That's a non-negotiable for me. I will never compromise on serving others.

When I see these hipster restaurants where you feel like you're privileged just for them to be serving you, I learn a lot about what I don't want to do. I think people will tire of that. I think when the cool factor wears off, what you're going to be left with was how you were treated. And I do believe that's a phase in our industry. It might be a ten-year phase (laughs), but I do believe it's a phase. We just opened O-ku in Charlotte and it's very, very busy, and people are, over and over again, talking about the service, the service, the service. I'm starting to see where people are starting to go, "Hey, we want to be treated nice again." I don't care if the chef has a bunch of tattoos and they're playing rap music while I'm eating. Yeah, the space is cool and it's packed and everybody wants a beer, but I want to at least feel like the people are glad I'm there.

On the other side of that, I see a lot of very creative ideas and things that I wouldn't have thought of. It's fun to watch. There's something to be learned, concepts that five, six, seven, eight years ago, people would not have resonated with. There's a restaurant here called Xiao Bao Biscuit. It's an Asian restaurant that was opened in a gas station. The chef is American and his wife is from Vietnam and they opened this small plate Asian place. They're in a huge spread in *Bon Appétit Magazine* this month. From a cuisine point-of-view, the lines have gotten really blurred. There are people that are opening Southern restaurants and they've got kimchi on the menu. There's this blurring of the lines, and the food press seems to love those kinds of places. It's a very interesting time in our business. But ***good service is timeless***. I think people will come back for it over and over again. It's what makes people feel good. And I don't think that's going to go out of style. I hope it doesn't.

What do you love most about this business?

The most rewarding thing for me is our people. There's nothing more rewarding for me than an employee that loves coming to work every day. There's just not. Having them genuinely like and notice and care and say, "I just love being at this restaurant." It's creating opportunities for people. At the end of the day I've never lost the enthusiasm for just taking care of people. And when people stop me and say, "Man, we had the best meal at so-and-so the other night," I just I love it. There's no more rewarding feeling for me.

What would you tell somebody that's looking to get into the business?

I would say to somebody that wants to own a restaurant, "Go work in one first." No matter if it's for six months or a year, just go wait tables. Even if you've been successful in some other business. There are two kinds of people that get into the business that haven't come up through the ranks. There's pure investors — and I have those and they leave me alone to run the day-to-day. So, that's one kind of ownership. They see it as a business opportunity and I think all of the folks that have been kind enough to invest in me have some level of romanticism about the industry. But then I see people that had never been in it and they have put their money in it and then they want to be hands-on with it, with no experience. I'm not going to say that you can't be successful, because I know people that have been. If you're going to get into the business with no previous work experience, make sure you're hiring the right people, the people that have been at it a long time, and then allow them to do their job.

The restaurant business from an investment point-of-view can be a very painful one. Our failure rate is still pretty darn high. I see people that have invested in a restaurant and for whatever reason, they didn't do their homework on what kind of concept the market needed, or they hired the wrong chef or general manager, and it's a very painful, bitter experience for them. You absolutely have to love the business. *The restaurant business is a business for people that love it, period*. Because it is hard and you go through economic downturns, saturation or lack of staff. You better love it because it is a demanding, high-maintenance girlfriend. If you don't love it, it can be really tough.

Sup Dogs

TWO LOCATIONS - GREENVILLE AND CHAPEL HILL, NC

RESTAURANT OWNER SINCE 2012

Tell me about the background of Sup Dogs.

There's a misconception that you need a ton of money to start a restaurant. My little brother, Derek, borrowed some money from my dad, and some money from my granddad. They just had blind faith in my brother and his laser-focused, crazy, bullheaded, confident personality. He knew he wanted to open Sup Dogs, the coolest in specialty hot dogs, specialty burgers, beer, liquor — the coolest, most fun restaurant there is in a college town. He was able to pretty much nail that.

Then we got that nightmare phone call September 29, 2011. I was getting ready to go to my job working in radio in Washington, D.C. The phone rang at three in the morning. There was a house fire and he went in while the house was on fire. I mean, who goes into a house while it's on fire? My brother does. I would never do that, but that same sort of confidence and passion he had in opening a restaurant, that was his personality. He went in after his dogs and though you may have enough oxygen to go into a fire, you never have enough to come out. If anything's ever on fire, stay a million miles away from it. Luckily there were no burns on his body. He died of smoke inhalation.

When he passed away, it was really a testament to his staff that they were able to keep it going. There were four months between when he passed away and when my wife and I moved down to Greenville. *It is a testament to the staff* that they were able to keep the restaurant going.

What made you decide to carry on his legacy? You had no restaurant experience, right?

Zero.

I'll give you a brief timeline. He passed away in September 2011, then my wife and I got married three weeks later. We went on our honeymoon and then somewhere around Thanksgiving we thought about quitting our jobs and moving down to North Carolina with the hopes of carrying on Derek's legacy and his dream.

I worked in sports talk radio in the Washington, D.C. area. We broadcasted from the Super Bowl in Indianapolis February 2nd, I believe it was. Then, on February 4th two days later, the moving trucks came and we moved down to random college town, Greenville, NC, right across the street from ECU (East Carolina University).

My brother was able to make such a cool restaurant and make it popular with the students. That was just his personality. He was always the funniest guy in the room, the best-looking guy in the room, the best personality in the room. So, making that restaurant awesome was easy for him. There's also the business side of things, which is controlling costs — labor costs, food costs, liquor costs, managing a staff and so forth. That wasn't really his strong suit. Even though we did have a great core of staff there, the operational side of things when my wife and I arrived was in disarray.

Tell me about those early days.

I had no idea what to do. Like, zero. I didn't even know how to tap a keg. I didn't know anything about the restaurant business. My wife, luckily, had been waiting tables her whole life, in and out of college. She had an idea from a server standpoint. I had no idea. I'm thirty-three now — I was thirty at the time. *My mentality was to just to outwork everyone, outlearn everyone, and ask every stupid question there is.* I figured I would just to be the biggest village idiot for a long time. But eventually, I'd know more than everyone.

I remember asking our food distributor, the beer reps, the liquor reps, people at my first trade show the world's worst questions, to the point where these people were like, "Wow, this idiot, he's out of his league here." That was my mentality. A few weeks into it, I just came home one day saying, "I don't know if I can do this. I don't know what to do. I don't know where to start." The restaurant was running and there were a lot of people in there, but I knew that it wasn't running optimally. I didn't know what to do or where to start. My wife just said, "Stop being a wimp. Go in. Walk around. Walk up to tables. You'll know immediately if they want to talk to you or not. And, just talk to them. Ask them if they need anything. Get a refill. Run food. Do whatever you can to just be around and talk to people. Talk to the staff." I said, "Okay, I'll try that."

I think it took about a year for me to really sort of have the confidence to run the restaurant. It was definitely tough and it was definitely weird. I thought our worst-case scenario was if my wife and I hate it, or the business fails, we would move back to D.C. That's what was running through my head at the time.

As you gained experience and confidence, what did you learn that helped you improve operations?

My biggest nightmare would be to be incredibly busy in the restaurant business and not make any money. That would be a total disaster. I'd rather just sit at home and do nothing. I mean, you've worked your ass off, there's a ton of people in your restaurant and there's no money to show for it. That would be a total nightmare. It was a little like that when I got there, because the restaurant was always busy but there wasn't a lot of money in the bank account. I think our menu was a little underpriced, and our labor costs were a little out-of-control. Food, beer, liquor costs needed to be sort of reined in. Even over three years into this thing, every day I think about how we can improve but at the same time save money, because saving money is like making money. But, *I never wanted to be one of those restaurant owners that are just cutting costs just to try to save a dime. I want to be improving.*

Here's a good example: we have a couple specialty hot dogs and nachos and burgers that we put jalapenos on. Everyone knows what a pickled jalapeno is that dark green jalapeno that you get out of the jug. To me, this just didn't look that good. I said, "Hey, what if we switched to a fresh cut jalapeno? It's a bit brighter, it's better looking, it tastes better, it's more fresh. And then, lo and behold, it's forty percent less expensive than if you just buy these jalapenos out of the jar." We were able to switch to a fresh cut jalapeno, improve our food and cut our costs. There's always a thousand ways to do that. You've really just got to dig and dig and figure out how it relates to your concept. I've been able to do that in a bunch of different ways.

When I first arrived, there was no portion control. The processes were not really in place to run a successful restaurant. At one point my brother was cooking the food, running the food to the table, greeting the customer — really doing it all. As a restaurant grows, it can easily start to get out of control. The processes aren't in place, you don't have time to implement them, and it swallows you up. I think there was a little bit of that going on with my brother. I guess that is a good problem to have — too busy, too many customers. When I got there, there were a lot of processes that needed to be in place.

Were there any resources that really helped?

I'm a fan of everything Schedulefly does. Within the first month of getting into the restaurant business, I bought your book Restaurant Owners

Uncorked. I've read the whole thing because it's all about successful restaurant owners. For me it was like, "I've got to figure out how to act like one, so let's read about the dude from Top of the Hill, Scott Maitland. Let's see how other restaurant owners act successfully and let me try to be a part of that." That book was actually the first one that I bought. I don't know how I really stumbled upon it, but it helped. It definitely helped. I still have it.

As is clear from your book, I don't think there is any one correct way to operate a restaurant. I've met a lot of restaurant owners who take a my-way-or-the-highway approach. And then you have a lot who are way too trusting and lenient. I'm kind of somewhere in-between. I do have a harder time delegating, and I seem to try to want to do everything myself. Now that we have a bunch of full-time managers and general managers, I've gotten a little better at delegating, but it's something that I'm working on.

There's definitely no right way. You have to figure out what works best. But there's so much you have to get right. Tell me more about your approach.

There's can be a dark side of restaurants. The booze, and a lot of times drugs, just cash everywhere. That can swallow you up. But my mentality was I want to run this like I'm running Apple. It sounds stupid, but *I'm going to run this tiny restaurant in Greenville like I'm running a Fortune 500 company*.

I wanted a legit restaurant with all the processes in place — everything from holding staff accountable to literally every dollar we bring in, we report. I've been told I'm crazy but every dollar that comes into the restaurant gets reported to our accountant and we pay taxes on it. I want to run this like any other successful company, not just a restaurant.

I wanted to make it successful but I have a bigger vision than one restaurant in Greenville, NC, even though it's awesome and I can live off that and be perfectly happy the rest of my life. What comes along with that is running a hundred percent legit business.

Tell me your second location in Chapel Hill.

We opened nine months ago. When I moved down here, there was so much I had to learn, and so much that I wanted to improve and change from a business standpoint that the thought of opening a second restaurant didn't cross my mind for a long time. My wife will tell you, we didn't talk about opening a second one for maybe a year-and-a-half, two years. Then we started kind of thinking about it. We started talking about where we would want to open a second one. It was always my brother's dream to open as many Sup Dogs locations as possible.

And you stayed with the college town concept?

Exactly, yes. College towns. The easy part would be to open up another Sup Dogs in Greenville and do it all locally. But we decided to look around. We found an awesome building in Chapel Hill, right on Franklin Street, right across from Top of the Hill. It was one of those things where it kind of just hit us like, "We can't pass up this space."

The process of starting a second restaurant is not easy, especially finding a prime location. We knew we wanted to be in an awesome downtown area and a great college town. There's very few college towns, if any, better than Chapel Hill. When we found that building, the next question was, "Okay, how can we convince this broker and landlord to lease it to us?" They wanted a business like Chipotle in there. That's where it really helps running a buttoned-up business, when trying to open that second one. All of our accounting was right. There was money in the bank. There are a lot of restaurants that try to start their second location, but their accounting is a disaster. There's no money. They've taken out money to go buy a boat and there's no money in the bank. We were able to keep a lot of that money in the bank. It helped a lot being able to show the broker and the landlord, "Hey, we've got a little bit of money. Hey, here's our balance sheet."

You really need to have to have a bigger mentality than, "I'm going to be one of those restaurant owners who's at the corner of the bar, drinking Jack and Coke and glad-handing people." I never eat or drink in the restaurant unless I have family or friends in town. They all eat at Sup Dogs when they visit. But overall, what I say is, "Look, is this party time? Or are you running a business here? Are you trying to make a million dollars?" That's my mentality.

For a lot of restaurant owners and bar owners, it is party time. You're drinking beers with your staff, you've got five thousand in cash in your pocket. You say, "Hey, let's go on a cruise — let's go to Las Vegas." But, when we moved down, I knew we wanted to have a bigger vision than just one restaurant. We took a huge pay cut in taking over Sup Dogs. For me, it was not all about how much money is in my bank account. I didn't really care just as long as I could pay bills. *I wanted to keep score by seeing how we could grow our restaurant's bank account.* That helped a ton in being able to get a little bit of loan money from the bank for our second location and establishing financing. You've got to make sure all your financials are legit or there's no chance of expanding. We were able to do that. We really just had the business in mind first.

Talk about the challenges of going from running one location to running two.

It's really hard. It's a grind. Having one restaurant is not easy — having two is twice the headaches, twice the risk. We bought a house here in Greenville, but we've also, for the last year-and-a-half, had an apartment in Chapel Hill. What's big for us in our concept is that we're a part of the University. We get to become a great part of the downtown area. I didn't want people asking me all the time, "Oh, is this a chain?" Especially in Chapel Hill, where they are a lot less familiar with our concept. They'll come in and ask if we are a chain. I take that as a compliment because to them maybe it looks like there's process in place to look like a chain, which is cool. But for us, I wanted to be local. It's important in markets like Chapel Hill, where if you're not a part of their community and you're not a part of the University, I don't think you're going to stand much of a chance unless you're a Chipotle, a Panera or something like that.

I'm probably in Chapel Hill three or four days a week. I'm here in Greenville two or three days a week. Really, I take zero days off. I might go out to dinner with my wife. You can't really have any hobbies. It might sound miserable but it's not. *You really have to be focused and be a part of the community in each of your restaurants.* In Greenville I'm always texting with the mayor. My wife's on the board for Uptown Greenville. So, we're super established in everything that goes on in Greenville, and we're slowly getting that way in Chapel Hill. It's not easy. You can't be in two places at once. But I want people to know this is a local restaurant.

Top of the Hill is part of the Chapel Hill community, through and through. We need a little bit of that in order to be a part of the community. I tell people all the time, "Hey, I live here." I literally live in Chapel Hill four days a week. We're not just opening up and sort of forgetting about it, saying "Okay, where's the next one?" It's not like that. It's really getting in there, grinding, getting to know your customers, getting to know other business owners, getting to know the city, going to all the meetings, and everything that goes into being a part of the community.

24

What's the biggest lesson you've learned from expanding?

You really have to stick to who you are. I know who we are. We are specialty hot dogs, specialty burgers, cheesy tots, cheesy fries. We are here for the college students. We are high energy, loud, bright, fun. We open up in college towns. College is fun, so our business is going to be fun. I want it to be the most fun. It's unorthodox, different from any restaurant. It's half restaurant, half just exciting party. It's a cool concept. But you've got to stick to who you are.

In Chapel Hill, our building looks awesome from the outside. We put a ton of money into it. So, it was weird because I think people were expecting some crazy, upscale burger bar with forty-five craft beers and Makers Mark on the shelf. It took us a while to find our audience. And there's pressure to conform to the norm and conform to what other people are doing. You really have to stick to what you do and what we do is for the college students. We make no bones about it. That's hard, especially when you move into a market where nobody knows you. There's tons of pressure to conform. You've got to know who you are and really fight and stay with who you are. Otherwise, I don't think you have a chance to be successful if you're opening a second one.

You also have to be patient. It takes a long time. We've been open for a little over nine months in Chapel Hill, and I feel like we're just starting to really find our audience and our customer base. We don't have a hostess. It's loud. It's bright. All of our servers are college girls. We are a little edgy, but nowhere near Hooters or any of these crazy restaurants. We're different from anything in Chapel Hill. It takes a long time just to build your brand and stick to your guns. It's tough, though. There are days where you're taking a beating. But in the end if you have all your processes in place and your product is there, I think you're going to be successful. I believe in what we do and I'm going to work as hard as I can possibly work. To me, that's a recipe for success. But, wow, there's a lot of pressure to be like everyone else. I have zero interest in doing that. It's definitely a battle and a grind, what we do every single day.

One of my favorite business books is called *Different: Escaping the Competitive Herd*. It's written by a marketing professor at Harvard, Youngme Moon. She talks about how important it is to take a stand and to be different if you want to create something special.

I totally agree. I think a lot of that applies to what we're doing. College is the most fun time in your life, so I want to be the most fun restaurant out there.

You have to know who your audience is. I think one of my strengths and my wife's strengths is knowing what college students in a college community want. We do get a ton of families in for lunch and a ton of families in for dinner. It's not just college kids that come into our restaurant. But when I think about college, it's all about girls and having fun. That's what our business has to be all about.

Our hotdog is six inches long, but it's not too thick. It's not like you're eating some big, giant hotdog at the stadium. Our patties are hand-packed fresh, hand-smashed. We smash them out real thin. To me, it's a little easier for a girl to eat it. A group of college girls isn't going to want eat a big, giant piece of cow before she goes to a house party with her friends. Everything we do is sort of with the college girl in mind — everything from our drinks to presentation of our food to the décor of the restaurant. My mentality is that if you can be successful doing that, the guys will follow and the community will follow. If I visit a college town, I want get a college experience.

We went to the University of Florida a couple years ago to go to football game and I wanted to see my wife's whole college experience. I wanted to be around the students — I wanted to be around the Gators. We get complaints: the restaurant's too loud, it's too bright, there are too many girls in there. They say, "Your staff act like sorority girls." Well, this is college. I mean, what do you want? I saw one Yelp review where some guy was like, "The food was great and the service is good, but their staff is laughing and they're loud and they're having fun. This isn't a sorority house, girl. This is work." I'm thinking, "This dude just doesn't get it."

Ninety-nine-point-nine percent of the stuff I hear is positive, and I love it. With complaints, my dad always says, "If there's someone that really doesn't like being there, it's like having a remote control. You could turn the channel if you want." There are always other options. You're not going to be for everyone, that's for sure.

If we make a mistake, or we're in the wrong, I am over-the-top apologetic. I'll do anything I can to make it right. *But my mentality, first and foremost, is to side with our restaurant and our staff, because most of the time they know what they're doing*. Those are the people you are working with, day-in and day-out. I really side with our staff first, but if there is stuff that comes up and if we mess up a ticket or the ticket time's thirty minutes or whatever it is, then I'm the first one to apologize. I know when we're in the wrong. But there is something to be said for sticking to your business and your staff and your beliefs.

Your passion is palpable. How do you motivate your team?

I always tell our staff, "We have to be the best." I try to instill that in them. I always try to tell them that we are the best and we have to be the best with everything we do. We're doing hot dogs and burgers and cheese fries, but I think it would be tough to find a restaurant that puts as much effort and time into presentation as we do. It's kind of ridiculous, but if you were in our kitchen you might see one guy correcting another guy because he didn't drizzle the ranch right on the Ranchero Dog. All of that stuff is really important, and that goes into taking pride and doing things the right way. I often tell our staff, "Look, there's a right way to do things and then there's a gray area. And we've got to be out of that gray area. We've got to do things the right way every single time."

Also, it takes time. We're starting to develop that in Chapel Hill. We're starting to develop that pride in our staff. You're starting to see less turnover. At first, that's rough. When we started our second location, certain staff members didn't really have pride in the concept. They didn't care about working, they didn't really care about the restaurant. Over time, you figure out who your key players are. In Greenville, people inherently take pride in working at Sup Dogs. Our staff is paid pretty well. Our girls make a ton of money. They work their asses off for it — nobody works harder than our servers. Making a lot of money goes along with that. Everyone's working so hard I feel like I'm running a sweatshop some days. I'm not kidding. *It's just so hard and so intense. But along with that comes pride and a sense of accomplishment every day*. I try to pay our cooks and our managers as much as I possibly can. We don't have anyone making minimum wage right now, including our busboys and dish guys.

Are you planning to expand to additional locations?

That's the really tough part. I don't think about it that much, to be honest with you. My mentality is making sure our Greenville location is as great as it's ever been, and only improves. I always want to get better. At our UNC location, I want to make sure we're established as a member of the community, and it's as profitable and is running about as well as it can.

Maybe we'll open a third. Maybe we just have two and I'm perfectly content with having two the rest of my life. Maybe one of them fails. Maybe both of them fail — I don't know. I don't take for granted that people are coming through the door. In my mind, I'm like, "*This whole thing could go away tomorrow*." I think about it a lot. Is this as good as it gets? Can we only go downhill from here? Every day I'm working to try to get better and to really just try to stay out in front of ourselves. I just don't take for granted that we're making money and we're busy and we have a great staff. With that being said, we have a thousand issues. I'm dealing with a billion staff issues right now. I'm dealing with food distributor issues. I'm out here, I'm fighting for money and staff issues and this and that. It's not all roses. It can be a total grind.

I've been doing this for about three years. I might come off sounding like I know a lot. I know I don't know hardly anything compared to most people. I look at a lot of restaurant owners, like Scott Maitland from Top of the Hill and a lot of these restaurant owners that you interview, and they're way ahead of me. I don't feel like I know everything. I might try to come across that way to our staff, but I know there's so much that I have no clue about. I look forward to learning that. I don't want people to think I'm some know-it-all, because I know there are people who have been in this business for twenty years and they know a billion times more than I do. For example, I found something out with our food distributor a month ago which made me feel like an idiot. I should have known this two years ago. Every day I find things out like that.

Chai Pani Restaurant Group

FIVE LOCATIONS ACROSS FOUR CONCEPTS -
ASHEVILLE, NC, ATLANTA AND DECATUR, GA

RESTAURANT OWNER SINCE 2009

Tell me about your background.

I'm from India, and I came to the U.S. when I was 20 to get an MBA. After grad school I moved to San Francisco to be with Molly, who I had met while working at a restaurant in Myrtle Beach, SC at my first job in America. I accidentally ended up in the auto industry working for Lexus. I thought it would be a part-time gig that I'd do for about six months, because my goal was to go back to college and get a degree in Computer Science. Instead, I fell in love with the business and ended up staying with Lexus for five years and then with Mercedes Benz for three years. I started off in sales and then worked my way up into management, and then finally upper management.

In 2002, Molly and I'd had our little girl. I was managing a fairly large division and she was working full-time because we were in San Francisco and unless you made millions of dollars out there, you were just getting by. We were completely in the rat race. I would leave for work at six in the morning to beat traffic, and my daughter would be sleeping. I would come home at ten at night — my daughter was again asleep. One day, Molly looked at me and said, "We can't do this anymore. We're missing our kid's childhood. She's being raised by babysitters." So we did that cliché thing where we sort of looked at each other and said, "Well, what if there's a small town somewhere that's still cool and hip and progressive and reminds us a little of San Francisco, but it will be affordable enough that Molly could quit her job and I'd find something to do, and we could raise our family." So, literally, we Googled "small cool towns in America to live and work". Along with a few of the usual suspects back then like Austin, Portland, and a couple of others, Asheville, North Carolina popped up really high on the list. And what ended up making it a reality was complete serendipity. Literally a day later I was talking to an old time friend who's in the real estate industry, and I mentioned casually that we were checking out Asheville. He said, "That's so funny! I was just talking to a real estate developer who's looking for a good guy to be in sales and marketing. If you're thinking of Asheville I could connect you two together." Well, five days later, we moved lock, stock and barrel.

The developer was buying tracts of land outside of Asheville and building second-home luxury gated communities with golf courses. It was perfect. We loved the town, we loved the people. And then 2009 happened. The market crashed and literally my developer went from millions of dollars in sales to facing bankruptcy in less than six months. Molly and I were driving back from a visiting her family and then she looked at me and said, "What are we going to do?"

30

Is that when you thought of starting a restaurant?

Well, that question sure got us thinking about every option.

A little background … You'll find that most immigrants like me from countries like India or Mexico or Asia come to America and we tend to start learning how to cook — even the men, even if they come from a culture where mostly the women cook. Because although you can go to an Indian restaurant here and there, for the most part *if I want to eat my country's food on a regular basis I'd better learn how to cook it* quickly. I used to cook at home and started cooking mostly Indian food. I was cooking in college while I was getting my MBA, and everybody knew when I was cooking and the next thing you know there's a crowd eating, or I'm always cooking at parties.

Then when I got to San Francisco, I started going to some really good restaurants and started expanding my repertoire. Literally, living there for ten years was an education in not just becoming a foodie but also in learning how to cook. I also just went naturally in and out of the restaurant world. My mother-in-law was a restaurateur and she had sold a restaurant to move to California, and then she was dating a guy that was a chef and he'd cook a lot and I'd hang out with him and I knew a little bit of the behind-the-scenes of the restaurant world. Whenever I was at a restaurant and had a chance to meet the chef or go in the kitchen, that's what I'd do. People laugh when I say this, but I learned a lot from watching Food Network. Back then it was before Rachel Ray and all that. It was back when they still had Jacques Pépin and Julia Childs on TV. You could actually learn something from watching them cook. That was it – books, the internet and TV.

Fast-forward back again to 2009 and Molly's asking me what turned out to be a pivotal question: "For the last fifteen years you've enjoyed what you did. You were good at it, but you never jumped out of bed saying, 'I can't wait to get to work today.' Maybe this is a sign. Maybe this is your chance to do something different."

Now, of course, we were both forty so this is like a classic mid-life crisis moment, right? But *if I could do anything I wanted to do, I wanted to cook*. We talked about me maybe going back to the Culinary Institute of America and getting a culinary degree. Then I would actually think this through and go, "Right, and then I'll be a ten dollar an hour line cook for eight years working for some asshole chef that's going to be yelling at me the whole time, and I'm forty and I can't compete with a twenty-year-old."

I'm thinking, "That's the stupidest idea in the world." So that was the end of that conversation.

You hear this other cliché that if something just percolates in your subconscious for a while and you're ready to do that, sometimes something awesome can pop up. Two weeks later I'm laying in bed reading a book at eleven-thirty at night with Molly by my side and I just sit bolt upright, and say, "Wait, I don't need to go work as a cook at somebody else's restaurant. I can open my own restaurant and do my own thing and pay myself what I want." She looks at me like, "What the hell does he know about opening restaurants?" Well, I may not know a lot about restaurants but I know a hell of a lot about business and sales and marketing. I said, "I think we can do this." I still had to write a hundred-and-fifty page business plan to convince her that we'd actually make money doing it. But that's kind of how it started.

150 pages?

Yeah, I went a little nuts. For awhile I was really worried about this sort of myth or urban legend that 70% - 90% (depending on who you ask) of restaurants go out of business in their first five years. I was really curious to find out if this is real or is this just an urban legend. I did the research. The University of Florida had a hospitality management program where they'd done a study on restaurant closings. They listed five reasons why a typical restaurant would close. They had the stats on restaurant failure rates. I think what they said was that a third of the restaurants close in their first year - the ones that don't close in the first year usually make it to their fifth year. That's when the second third closes, for completely different reasons than the first year.

But, their point was that there are all the usual suspects for why a lot of restaurants goes out of business – lack of capital, bad food, bad market conditions, location. But all of those are completely eclipsed by the single, most overriding factor, and that was *lack of a defined concept that is easy to articulate*. If somebody asked you what kind of restaurant it was, the key was in being able to answer that question as simply and quickly as you can. And the study went on to say that's why even mom-and-pop Mexican restaurants in strip malls and Chinese restaurants and Italian restaurants all tend to last, even the ones that aren't that good. One thing they have going in their favor is when somebody says what kind of food it is – you can just say "Chinese" and that's it. But when you have a restaurant going, "Well, we do a fusion of Mediterranean-Tapas-style but with a little bit of Asian ingredients and . . ." Yeah, you lost me. That was their point. So that was a key factor in my business plan — I wanted to make sure my concept made sense.

When did you open Chai Pani?

Today's our to-the-day six-year anniversary — September 23, 2009. We were supposed to be open this day six years' ago from 11am to 11pm, but we ran out of food at two o'clock. I had to shut the doors. We had opened the doors to literally a line around the block, and by the second day there was a TV crew inside because they had no idea what the hell was going on and why there were lines around the block. On the second day, we ran out at four o'clock. On the third day we had to shut down because we had no food left to even cook. We had to go buy food and prep it.

We opened the restaurant for seventy thousand dollars, and the only money that left was two-hundred-and-fifty dollars in the cash register. I knew that if we didn't sell enough of our food in the three days, I wouldn't have enough money to buy more food or even make payroll for that first pay period. That's how close we cut it.

How did you finance the restaurant?

Again, this is the middle of the recession of 2009. Lehman Brothers had gone under. Merrill Lynch got sold out. The market was a disaster and no bank was giving money to anybody. We went to a local bank, and they just as kindly as they could, they said, "Meherwan, (A) we're not loaning money to anybody, (B) restaurants are a disaster - you know, we don't normally give money to restaurants in the best of times, and (C), Indian street food? You're in a town of a hundred thousand where ninety-nine thousand people are white. People barely know what Indian food is, let alone Indian street food." And that was the end of that conversation.

Then I went to the SBA. Then I went to these microloan organizations that said they help businesses. Everybody was impressed with the hundred-and-fifty page business plan, but at the end of the day, they'd say, "No, we can't give you the money." Molly was adamant that we not leverage our house because it was, at this point, the only asset we still had. So I wrote an open letter to all my friends and family, anybody that was close to us, and I kept it open - I didn't actually email it to people individually with their name. I just sent it as a blind email to all of my contacts. "If you're getting this letter and you don't respond, I won't know. This is what we're doing and this is what we believe in and if you believe enough and believe that we can pay you back, anything you can give will be appreciated." And the checks started coming in the mail – seventy-five dollars, two thousand dollars, three hundred dollars.

Then the pivotal check came. A friend of ours, a young man named Isaac Clay who's now the general manager at Chai Pani in Decatur, GA and a partner in the business, was teaching at the local high school here. He'd been to India a number of times. He said, "Hey, I heard you were trying to raise money for this Indian street food idea. I'd been thinking that I would want to open that kind of restaurant because I think it's a good idea." I'm like, "Oh no - well, sorry, Isaac. I didn't mean to step on your toes. I had no idea that you'd want to do something like that." He said, "No, no. I could never open a restaurant. I'm here to give you a check." I think Isaac was twenty-four at the time, and like I said, a teacher at the public high school. He wrote a check for twenty-five thousand dollars. At that time, it was the difference between we can do this and we can't do this.

I was dumbfounded. (A) how did you get this much money? (B) this must be every penny you own. I think in that moment it established the first cultural touchstone of Chai Pani — the notion that *we believe in people more than we do in money*. Because, really, at the end of the day, Isaac had to believe in me - not my idea - to give me that money. I looked him in the eye and said, "I will pay you back."

Then the ball kind of got rolling. A few more people came up with the rest. We, of course, maxed out our credit cards and emptied our bank accounts. Then we started looking for a spot. There was this little business downtown that was going under and a new owner from Atlanta had purchased the building (Sammy Rawlins, who is my landlord to this day). My broker told me this before the building went on the market. I figured if I could get a jump on this and talk to him right away, he might give me the space.

He was just a wonderful sweet guy, old school gentleman from Atlanta that had made his money in the plumbing business. I think he had had Indian food once in his life. So at our meeting he's looking at me and he's asking me about my experience in the business and I'm like, "Well, none really. I waited tables." He asked where I got my training as a chef. "Well, actually, I'm self-taught." He asked, "How much money do you have for working capital?" We had none. All we had was what we had to open the restaurant with.

(Laughing) What do you think it was that convinced him to take a chance with you?

He said, "Tell me why you want to do this. What do think the numbers will look like?" I showed him my business plan, and Molly and I talked to him for a while, and that evening I sent him an email acknowledging how crazy this must seem. On the surface it looked like a mistake. It's this amazing spot in downtown Asheville. He could have leased that thing in a heartbeat to anybody in town. So when I emailed him I thanked him for being with me and just gave him one last pitch. A few days later he called us up and said he wanted to give us the space. When I asked him why, he said I reminded him of him a little bit in the sense that I did my homework — I had my business plan — I talked through the numbers. He also said, "At the end of the day *you followed up*. Somebody does that, they have what I believe it takes to be successful in any business." All those years of being in the sales business helped pay off with just a simple follow-up to say thank you to somebody.

What was your expectation before you opened?

So of course, everybody else is looking at this plan like I was insane. But I knew that this would be a hit. Asheville was on the cusp of this burgeoning food scene. I looked around the town and I saw people like myself and Molly. Essentially, young couples moving here from big cities like Seattle, Portland, Atlanta, San Francisco and L.A. — all doing what we were doing — trying to find a town that was sort of progressive, in the mountains, hip and cool. It was a great town in 2009 to just be — where there wasn't the pressure of, like, "Oh, my God, I graduated college and now I have to go find a job somewhere." It was the kind of town where artists, and hippies, and people that were just taking a break from life were hanging out because it was affordable and there was a cool vibe to the town.

So I knew the market was there. I knew there were enough people around us to make this thing happen. In my mind I'd be in the kitchen, Molly would be behind the register, and my daughter would be in the corner doing her homework. Your classic immigrant family opens a restaurant. And most importantly, we'd be happy. If I was happy, Molly would be happy and Aria would be happy. So, that was the plan. But I also knew that there was potential for this to get busy because this was the kind of town that would love the idea of Indian street food. It sounded different, it sounded exotic.

The second thing that happened was all those friends and family that all gave us money, and plenty that didn't give us money, showed up to help work. Friends from California, friends from around town, friends from Atlanta said, "Hey! Late summer, we're going to be in Asheville and we'd love to come and help you put this thing together."

It went from *the start-up of a business to kind of like community work*. It's almost like building a house for a family. That's what it felt like. We couldn't even pay people. Even the people that we had to pay, we were giving them five or six bucks an hour, and then giving them something as a credit towards food at Chai Pani for life, and/or maybe a future paycheck if we ever made money.

Well, those guys have their circles of friends and their circles of friends have their circles of friends. Social media was just starting to take off. Twitter was starting to become what it is today. It was literally one hundred percent word-of-mouth. We opened in September and by December of that year, the local newspaper ran a list of the most mentions on social media and events or incidents in Western North Carolina and the opening of Chai Pani was the number one most tweeted, blogged or written about event in Western North Carolina. So, yes — my instincts were right. People showed up. I mean, way more than I thought they would.

And now it's six years later and you have multiple locations and a highly-respected brand. What's working?

I read something that some business guy — could have been Warren Buffet or could have been Steve Jobs, or someone like that — basically said there are certain commonalities to successful businesses that are started from scratch. The three most important things that they have in common are, number one, somebody with a very clear vision and a sense of purpose. Number two, people that were willing to completely buy into that vision. Almost like tribal loyalty buy-in. And three, limited resources. In fact, *scarcity of resources*. The first two make sense. But the third one really struck the deepest.

I did have this real clear sense of what I wanted to do. And when I explained it to people I knew they bought into the vision — or maybe they were buying into me. In either case, they believed in something. But the critical factor was that our limited resources made us really think outside the box and forced us to do things differently because we didn't have the money to do it the way we were supposed to. For example, opening with two hundred and fifty dollars in the cash register and not even having enough money for payroll and using social media instead of putting ads in the local paper. We couldn't afford to advertise at all. Period. Zero. None. Yet at the same time, anytime a charity approached us for any kind of benefit or to give food or to give gift cards or to come cook, we'd jump all over it. So now, six years later with four restaurants and a fifth on the way, we still do that. We don't advertise but we give tens of thousands of dollars a year of food or time or effort for charities.

So, those three ingredients combined created an environment that might have seemed extraordinary to you, but to us that was just the way we did things. That's how we're able to do it today.

It sounds like having all these people believing in you really motivated you.

Exactly. You have people that have not only loaned you money but they're then showing up every day to eat at the restaurant to support the business because they believe in it and they want it to be successful — not only because then they'd get their money back, but it just created this richer cycle, if you will, of basically goodwill within the community. This was our story, and we were very open with the town about it. It was no secret that this was how we raised the money to do this, because all our friends that were there, that loaned us money and were helping out, were telling their friends. Today you'd call it a Kickstarter campaign or crowdfunding. Well, this was pre-Kickstarter — this was our version of it and because it was so local it really did create a cycle of goodwill.

How have things changed as your business has grown?

Raising money is no longer an issue, thank God. Our first major national write-up was, again, probably serendipity. One-year-to-the-date almost after we opened The New York Times came to do a write-up on Asheville called the "36 Hours in Asheville." They do this all over the world — they spend thirty-six hours in a city and then they write up in the travel section of the Sunday edition of The New York Times. I know people that will use that as a reference guide for when they go to a city and do the things because The New York Times is so highly respected. So they came to Asheville and they wrote up their ten things to do in Asheville and they wrote up Chai Pani and I think they called us as a star in the downtown dining scene or something like that. That blew us wide open. We were getting calls from all over the country, with people calling to make reservations.

And Asheville's star was definitely rising. More and more people were coming to visit it. Many more tourists were coming, many more people moving here. It all collided perfectly and sort of created this perfect storm for Chai Pani to just reach a much broader audience than just the town. The more Asheville got written up, the more the magazines were coming in and looking for the cool businesses to talk about. The more we were perceived as cool, the more we got written up in the magazines like GQ and The Wall Street Journal and USA Today. It just snowballed on that first year. It was insane.

Is that when you decided to expand?

Well the offers started pouring in. Literally, once a week, I was getting a phone call from somebody that wanted to franchise or invest or open one in a new location. I was so unprepared for this. We were barely able to keep Chai Pani staffed and stocked and able to feed the amount of people that came through the door.

It took us four years to open the second one. Late 2012 was when we started looking at the second location in Decatur. At that point, raising some money to open that was just as simple as reaching back out to the people that had asked to invest to invest with us then. We're still what I would consider in a circle of family and friends, except they had bigger checks to write. That's how we opened the second one.

But, as far as our ethos, opening in the middle of a recession like we did was just a lesson that was instantly valuable because it just really taught me to look at numbers and how much it costs to open a restaurant and what it takes to do it differently than if we had gotten all that money upfront. So even with the new restaurants, *we still bootstrap it*. Take the least amount possible, have the least debt load in the business so that we can do things the way we want to do it and not be beholden to the balance sheet or to an investor payment schedule or anything like that.

With your growth you've had to expand your team and place a lot of trust in people. Tell me about that.

Yeah, absolutely. The first major expansion was Atlanta and it was a big jump. We went from a small forty-seat restaurant to a hundred-and-twenty-five seat restaurant in Decatur in a much bigger market. Before we opened, Atlanta Magazine called Chai Pani one of the most anticipated openings in Atlanta, and after we opened we were named one of the ten best new restaurants in Atlanta. We knew we were going into a much bigger, higher-visibility market. So, nine of our Chai Pani family uprooted themselves and relocated to Atlanta to help open it.

I call them my culture carriers because I wanted them to bring three-plus years of this culture that I built at Chai Pani to the new business there, even though we'd be hiring fifty-sixty new individuals. Some of them eventually came back because they were able to do their job and come back to Asheville, and some of them stayed on there. Three of the four original line cooks we hired here in Chai Pani Asheville are still with us. Daniel Peach, who was an original hire in Asheville is now the head chef in Decatur. He was just named "Thirty under Thirty Rock Stars" by Zagat magazine. James Grogan, who's since been written up in Savuer and Bon Appetit, remains here with me in Asheville and runs the kitchen program . That's kind of how we do it. Many times I will hire or hang onto to people even though I don't have a job for them. Even then, I might not necessarily be able even to afford to keep them on or to hire them, but I do it because I know that one day this person is going to be a rock star somewhere else.

It's easy to say, "Trust your people." You're probably familiar with Danny Meyer from Union Square Hospitality Group in New York. He's got this great book called Setting the Table. There are a couple ideas that I kind of stole from that book when we started really ramping up on hiring people. For instance, our application is probably the craziest application most people have filled out. We ask questions that make many people stop and go, "I've never been asked that on a job application before."

What I'm looking for is **empathy**. Do they actually understand how their actions make other people feel? Does this person have emotional intelligence? Can they communicate well and understand how emotionally-driven people are at the end of the day, and that how you motivate them is by connecting at that level?

For me, work ethic is not about how many hours somebody puts in or how hard they work. Work ethic to me is this inclination to always do something as well as it possibly could be done. Nothing less than that is acceptable. There are people all around us wired that way. So, we look for that combination and then I really, actually let them run with it. I go, "Hey, I would do no better or no worse than them in their shoes with the same decisions." I have trusted myself to figure it out and make the right decisions, so I've got to trust them, too. As long as I have my culture carriers in there, in the midst of them, I know, generally speaking, our culture will be intact. But I want to let these people make their own decisions. That's how Chai Pani Decatur runs — it's a completely autonomous business, and my job is just to inspire and not worry too much about micromanaging their decisions.

Tell me about how your new barbecue joint, Buxton Hall.

Again, it's about the people. One of the most talented chefs in this town, Elliot Moss, was the chef at a restaurant called The Admiral, which kind of blew up at the same time Chai Pani did. It went from being in a dive bar on the wrong side of the tracks in a concrete building to one of the most talked about and renowned gastro pubs in this region. It took two weeks to get a reservation and it was constantly being written up and received numerous accolades. He was also nominated by the James Beard Foundation for a Best Chef Award a few years ago. And one day I heard that he'd walked away from the Admiral and another project he was involved in. I had met him professionally through the circuit — we cooked a few events together. So I reached out to him. He said that the whole time at The Admiral he was not an owner. He was just the chef. But he had basically, in his words, been made a promise to have his own restaurant one day, and then that fell apart. It was going to be whole-hog, wood smoked Eastern Carolina-style barbecue. But the partnership fell apart and now he was on his own. I didn't know much about Eastern Carolina-style barbecue. I mean, when I first came to the South I would be grilling and say, "Hey, I'm having a barbecue. You guys want to come over?" Somebody would invariably correct me and say, "Look. Unless you shot a pig in the head and spent eight to eleven hours smoking it, it's not a barbecue — it's a cookout." I was like, "Right, okay. Got it."

But here's the thing. I recognized in Elliot that *same spark that I had in my eye* about Chai Pani before we opened, where I kind of get like a mad scientist look in my eye. He'd always have that look in his eye when he's talking about barbecue. He grew up in Florence, South Carolina, and he grew up eating Eastern Carolina-style barbecue. I was honest, "You know I have no idea what you're talking about." He said, "Well, let's do this. Why don't we go on a tour and I'll show you what I'm talking about." So we ended up renting a caravan, piled five of us in there, including a local food writer and a videographer, and we spent five days going through the Carolinas eating at some of the most iconic barbecue joints out there. When I came back not only did I have an education in barbecue, but I knew that I wanted to help Elliot open a restaurant.

We literally just fell into an easy sort of conversation about finding the space and helping him build this thing. Molly and everybody in my company were initially pretty confused, "Why are we getting into the barbecue business?" When I opened Chai Pani it was obvious I had to do Indian food — I had to do something I was interested in because I would be the most attentive to that. But, I love food. I would have just as happily opened an Italian restaurant if I were Italian. A Colombian restaurant if I was a Colombian. The point is that I love food and love other cultures and other food. And this guy was onto something amazing. I would go to those old school barbecue restaurants on our trip and see the lines of people outside these little shacks in the middle of nowhere, queued up for barbecue. I knew there was something going on at a *cultural level that runs deep*. The way it is for Indians when they come into Chai Pani and get tears in their eyes because they're eating the home cooked food that they hadn't tasted since they'd left India fifteen years ago. I wanted to tap into that. I believe in this guy and this vision. And that's what happened. It took us a year-and-half to put all the pieces together, but we finally did and Buxton Hall opened about three weeks ago.

I'm actually in Buxton Hall downstairs in the office talking to you and I can smell the wood smoke — our pits are all one hundred percent wood-fired. We're definitely the only place in Asheville that's figured out how to put the pits inside the building, and it helped that we found a ten thousand square foot ex-roller skating rink from the 1920s. Soaring high ceilings, with floor-to-ceiling windows that look out onto the mountains. You walk in, and between the look of the space, the open pits, and the smoke, you feel like you're stepping into something special. It's every foodie's dream come true. It's everything we ever hoped it would be.

Cantina 76

TWO LOCATIONS - COLUMBIA AND GREENVILLE, SC

Za's

COLUMBIA, SC

RESTAURANT OWNER SINCE 2009

42

How did you get started in the restaurant business?

We opened our first Cantina 76 location in November of 2009. We opened it because we had seen similar concepts, especially in the Atlanta area where my two of my business partners and I had lived for a number of years. We thought it would work well here in Columbia. It's kind of Southwestern TexMex cuisine with a little bit of an Americanized flair. We do things like barbecue brisket tacos, fried chicken tacos, your standard quesadillas, chimichangas, those type things. It's more of an a la carte menu, and then pick what you want. It's in-and-out fast. We try to provide a friendly, upbeat, lively atmosphere where people can enjoy some margaritas, and TVs if anyone wants to watch the game.

The last restaurant experience I'd had was back in college, fifteen-plus years ago. It was a little bit of a wing and a prayer when we decided to take the leap of faith. We had to believe that we had an idea that would work here and that we would be able, in the process, to figure out the rest in terms of what it took to get a restaurant up and running and then execute on our vision for the food and service elements, and manage to that. I wasn't someone who came from a career background in the restaurant business, but my business partners and I have kind of figured it out as we go along.

Did your business partners have more experience in the industry?

If not less, to be honest with you. I waited some tables and one summer in college I was a cook at a deli in Charleston, South Carolina. But I had forgotten most of what I had known, and my business partners were all successful in other areas — pharmaceuticals, a vice president of a steel company and one who owns his own financial advisory firm.

We had to rely on our business experience and trust that we were smart enough to figure out the rest. I think more than anything we believed in the concept. In order to have a successful business you first have to have a particular food that people want to eat. It sounds obvious but sometimes people try to just push a particular kind of food into an *area that may not be ready* for that particular quality or sophistication of food. That's our core value and we thought this would work in Columbia. Lucky for us it definitely did.

Tell me about your partnership structure.

We're all operating partners in a sense that we govern and run the business. We started the first Cantina 76 in 2009. I came onboard full-time and was the operating partner/general manager/manager/busboy/bartender – a little bit of everything. Obviously I worked with those guys in terms of how we should run the business, the ins and outs, particularly getting it open. The other three kept their day jobs. Then, almost two years ago, we expanded to our second Cantina 76 location, which is on Main Street a few miles away from our first location. One of my business partners, Chad Elsey, took the lead on that one, and came on board as the day-to-day operations manager while once again the other two gentlemen have kept up their career jobs to date. With eyes on expansion, we hope to bring those guys on in the near term as we transition to more restaurants, either in Columbia or the surrounding cities here in South Carolina.

It's kind of been a process where when it makes sense from the restaurant and/or the workload is there, that each of us have come onboard. At this point, it hasn't made sense for all of us to be full-time with the company. But again, those guys all have a hand in making the bigger decisions as to how the restaurants are run and the general direction of the company.

Without prior experience, there must have been a huge learning curve.

It was entirely learning on the job. It's funny when I think back to who I was as a restaurant owner, and in particular, who I was as a restaurant manager back in 2009 and probably a lot of 2010. It was fairly laughable to be completely frank. I worked long hours and I was willing to do every and anything from bartending to helping busboys bus tables and taking out the trash. But back then I absolutely wasn't the most effective manager. I was certainly trying to soak everything in that I could. It took time to evolve from someone who was completely green, trying to figure out the ins and outs of the restaurant business.

I learned from a few people. We were lucky in terms of, believe it or not, hiring some good college-age girls that had a lot of serving experience that I could kind of tap into for basic things like what we should do when we open the restaurant, how should we section the restaurant, how do we make cuts — things of that nature. More importantly, we were smart in that even though it was a "taco place" we went out and hired a very experienced executive chef, David Grillo. It was smart not only from a culinary standpoint - he had an absolute ton of talent - but he also had a long career, both with smaller restaurants as well as having worked previously with Appleby's and TGIFridays and a couple more corporate establishments where he was able to give me at least some direction as to how restaurants work, how restaurants are run, day-to-day operations and how they should go. Then there was all the back-end financial accounting, point of sale system and what spreadsheets to build out, what else to construct for your staff - a lot of that was just kind of left to me to figure out on my own and/or to do some research online. Along with being green in the business itself, we really didn't have a ton of contacts in the restaurant industry that we could rely on or use as a mentor. It was a lot of hard work and we made a lot of mistakes along the way. We learned from those mistakes and kept trying until we got it right.

What were some of those mistakes?

I would joke that I didn't even understand the concept of an expo act, an expo window, and what that person was supposed to do. You have the ability to pay and train an expo and staff an expo every night. I'd come in with all the drive and the hustle in the world but, it was me jumping behind the bar and me bussing tables and of course, touching tables and talking to customers that I felt comfortable with.

A lot of the mistakes were just not knowing what I could do as a manager to more effectively run a shift and make sure that the people that I employ were doing what they were supposed to be doing. You have a basic sense, obviously, from eating in restaurants all your life that the server's supposed to serve and somebody comes and cleans the table and when you walk in the door a host will seat you and if you go to the bar, the bartender serves the drinks. But you don't really understand the nuances of how to make those people work as a team and the little things that take a restaurant experience from *good to great*. That's probably where most of my mistakes were centered. Though, I'm sure, if you talk to former employees they'd probably have a longer list than I did. (Laughs)

How did you finance the business?

We funded it ourselves. With four of us that was kind of easier. It was interesting, too. In 2009 we were still obviously in the heart of the recession and our first location is in a spot that was a previous long-term restaurant that had existed for fifteen-plus years in the Columbia market. The particular building had been built so this restaurant could move from down the street into a bigger location. Another guy who owned that restaurant for a number of years sold it and the guy he sold it to didn't know what he was doing. So, they had run it into the ground in less than a year from a previous thirteen-year period of success. Then the property sat. Unlike today, where this property would literally be snapped up in probably thirty days or less, it sat for nine months, which allowed us to focus and take our time, write a business plan, do our research, and get our act together, so to speak. We were lucky enough to still have the property sitting there waiting on us. Believe it or not, the recession played a big part in that.

Coupled with that, we were a more reasonably priced restaurant option at that time. I think a lot of the restaurant business was moving to more affordable options as compared to fine dining places. Even though it was a recession and everyone was struggling, coming and spending ten to fifteen dollars on a taco meal was still feasible for most of the people out there.

Are there challenges with having four people involved in making decisions?

Absolutely. We fight sometimes like brothers and at times we look at each other and go, "God, if it was only me these decisions would come much more quickly and fluidly without half the discussions and arguments." But on the flip side, one of the things we've gotten very lucky with is that we're all four very diverse in our thinking and that creates for the discussion that ultimately leads to some great decisions.

The process definitely can be trying, but you look back and go, "Alright, that turned out to be a good decision and I don't know if I would have made that decision if it was just me. Yeah, there's *power in numbers*."

A prime example would be our second location. It literally is a few miles away, though in a different area of town, right on the Main Street business district high rise component of Columbia. You find very few restaurants – even the Chipotles and McDonald's of the world – that are putting restaurants that close. I don't think I would have made the decision on my own to feel confident in putting a restaurant that close. But with four guys that huddled up and said, "Hey, this is a different area, a different clientele, and for our restaurant business, this is where it needs to be. Let's do it." That one's been an absolute homerun as well. So, while there's a little bit of bad, there's a lot of good in terms of having the three guys do this with me.

With two successful Cantina 76 locations, when did you decide to open Za's?

Well, Za's was interesting. Za's was another restaurant that had been in existence for fifteen years and still had a loyal following. It's located directly across the street from our first Cantina restaurant. It was a long-term establishment but quite frankly as the years went on the owner hadn't put any money into it, hadn't improved on the property or the interior. His focus was definitely slipping, and consequently, from a sales perspective the business had started trending down.

We saw that as a really good opportunity. You have to be familiar with Columbia, but that restaurant and the first Cantina 76 are located on Devine Street, which is not too far from the University of South Carolina campus and is surrounded by neighborhoods. You get a lot of locals and people from the surrounding area, but people also come from all over to shop in that area or pass through to other parts of town. So, we saw Za's as a great opportunity. First of all, it was a great property. Second, though the business was starting to flounder a little bit, the sales numbers were there. If we could get in decent improvements with the interior and the food offering, we could get some of the people that we knew had not been going there as regularly and stop the trend of declining sales. We could turn it around to where we could grow the business and it wouldn't take us too long to get back to those numbers, and it would result in a very successful restaurant. We took a stab at that because it was a near-term opportunity and so far, so good.

Did not having much restaurant experience help in some ways?

Absolutely. Absolutely. I think with any business you come in and as you rise through the business, you take on the preconceived notions or ways of doing things - how the front of the house and the back of house never get along, for example. We were able to come in with a *different approach* of no-no-no - not in our restaurant. The front of the house and the back of house are absolutely going to get along. The kitchen can be friends with the servers and be friends with the bussers, the servers are going to get along with the bartenders, and so on. There was no tried-and-true brainwave of how we do things as it came to restaurants. I think that's helped us immensely in terms of coming in with a fresh outlook.

What have been the most important drivers of your success?

It's a few things. Obviously, the food is, in my opinion, is always first. You could have everything else in line but if your food's not good and it's not something that people want to eat then they're probably not going to return. Next comes service. You've got to have great food but you have to provide great service. Atmosphere is important as well. We weren't reinventing the wheel in terms of those things but I definitely think we execute on each one of those in a very fresh manner. The people we hire and people that had been long-term restaurant people were kind of refreshed in a sense and this was a new chapter in their careers. They liked the way we did things. It's a pretty obvious statement, but you're *only as good as the people that work for you*. I think we've been very lucky to be able to create a working environment where those people can excel.

What do you look for when you're hiring staff?

Back of the house, definitely we look for experience. It doesn't have to be tremendous. A lot of the people we've employed over the years are people who are in hospitality and management at the University of South Carolina - they've got a really good program. It doesn't have to be a tremendous amount of experience but obviously experience in the back of the house is desired.

Front of the house, you've got to have a good many experienced servers. When you have a strong core team you can build around that with some people that have less experience. If someone comes in and has a great personality and they pay their bills and pay their rent and need to work and are less concerned about going to a football game or out to the bars, you can go with someone that maybe has a little less experience and just train them really well to do the job. I think on the front of house side it's a little more of a balancing act of getting both the experienced people and some with a little less. As we've moved through the years we've come up with almost standard ways of bringing those people on who have less experience as hostesses so they can get a feel for how the restaurant works and ringing in to-go orders and then moving them on to servers as they gain that experience.

Has being in a college town been good for business?

Two of us are from Columbia and three of the four business partners went to the University of South Carolina years ago. We knew Columbia and we knew the University, but as far as USC, it's a university that five years' ago was twenty-eight thousand students and now I think it's up to probably the mid-thirties. The most interesting thing about being in a college town is if you can capture some of the college market, it provides a steady stream of potential customers. When a restaurant opens, if you like it you're there two or three times a week. Six months later, you might be eating there once a week. Six months after that you might be eating there once every two weeks, and then once every month. It's just the natural order of things that we get tired of places we go to over and over. The big advantage with USC students is when you hit that cycle then they graduate and you have a *perpetual new flow* of students coming in that can patronize your business. USC has been absolutely great to us. And we love the USC students, no doubt about it.

How have you spread the word about what you're doing?

It's definitely been through word-of-mouth. I won't say we've done no advertising, but we've done very little. It again goes back to good food in particular, and hopefully good service. People have been great in terms of spreading the word. We've gotten very lucky on that part. None of us are expert marketers. We did do a little campaign in 2010, where we spent some money in a mix of prints, some TV ads and radio ads. Looking back, we never got a sense as to whether or not that was truly effective and we haven't done any since because of that.

One of the things that was great is South Carolina has a thing called Restaurant Week where they do a state-wide branding and advertising of this thing and restaurants can participate. After our first year of operations things were going okay, but not great. We participated in Restaurant Week and just had an absolute ton of people through the doors. Going back to word-of-mouth, a lot of people left and went and told other people and from there the business kind of took off. I always give a lot of credit to our success to that first Restaurant Week we did back in 2011.

So your ad money is instead used on making a better guest experience to help foster word-of-mouth?

Absolutely. When you think about it, even the smallest ads in local magazines are really expensive. A lot of times if you're out spending a thousand dollars on an ad, you can spend a thousand dollars on a new TV - or if you're not spending X-amount on a radio spot, you can spend that on your stereo system or something along those lines. If you don't have a big ad budget, you can spend more on *your people*. If you want to hire a line cook that everyone else might pay ten dollars, you're able to pay eleven-fifty. So, you're able to get good people to execute on the food.

That's another thing. When you talk about the number one goal — providing good cuisine — well, you don't always have your chef there to make the food. He's training people too and he needs time off as well and so you've got to have great people that can consistently execute on the vision as well. Absolutely the lack of advertising has allowed us to be a little freer with our spending in other areas which is a definite benefit for the long-term success of the restaurant.

Do you plan to continue to grow one or both of the concepts?

Yeah. We're really more focused on the Cantina — that's our baby and that's definitely the concept that I think lends itself to expansion. We wouldn't have bought into another area if not for Za's being a place that we grew up on and knew very well and it being right in our wheelhouse location-wise. It's a great space that I really think we can utilize for years to come, even if Za's is not ultimately successful.

But we definitely are planning to grow Cantina. We've been looking for a while now for locations in Greenville, Charleston, and Lexington, which is an area outside of Columbia. I give major credence to our general luck with starting this thing back in the recession. It's the opposite these days in terms of the economy being so hot and restaurants popping up all over the place, especially in Columbia. That obviously ties up the real estate market and makes it a little more difficult to find that prime location. That's another thing that should be obvious that I don't think a lot of people execute on — you have to find a great location. If that requires a little more *patience*, then so be it. We started out with success at both places. It was definitely due to where the building is located and the surrounding opportunity in terms of the neighborhoods and students for the Devine Street location and the business clientele on Main Street.

How do you know when you've got a great location?

I don't know that you fully do until you open, to be honest. There's a lot of inherent risk in every restaurant decision you make, especially with the location. We just know the town of Columbia inside and out because we've either grown up here or been here a long time. Obviously, it'd be different with some of these other cities. One of our business partners is from Charleston and we all spend a good deal of time and have a number of friends in Charleston, so we have a good lead, I think, on what "great locations" may be there — areas that are up and coming and the more developed areas. If we choose to go to Greenville, quite frankly, it's going to be a little bit more of a challenge. We don't know as many people up there. We haven't spent as much time there.

Do you think that learning so much on-the-job helped you become a better leader?

Absolutely. The more you can do in a restaurant then the more you can coach on how to do that job in a restaurant. And just as importantly, the more you *understand the challenges* that those people face.

I'll give you a prime example. When you get busy as a bartender, sometimes you forget to ring in drinks. You have no understanding of why that happens - that it's not stealing, that it's not because they're not smart enough to do the job or capable enough to do the job. But, sometimes it just happens because you had all these people barking out drink orders at you and sometimes your focus isn't on something like, "I got to ring these in, ring these in, ring these in." It kind of changes the way you manage those individuals. You're not coming down as hard on them, like, "Gosh, you've got to ring in those drinks. I can't believe you failed at your job." It's more, "Hey, ring in those drinks - I know where you're coming from. I've been there." Absolutely, looking back, I was glad I did those things because it's given me a different perspective as a true manager of those people I employ now.

Paul Wise

Christianos Pizza

THREE LOCATIONS - GREEN LAKE, OSHKOSH AND
WAUTOMA, WI

RESTAURANT OWNER SINCE 2008

Tell me the story of Christianos.

My dad started it in '96. He had prior experience growing up in Milwaukee, working with some Italian families that ran restaurants. He got to the point in his life where he wanted to live out his passion, and that was always making pizzas. He thought, "Let's start a restaurant." I think I was ten or eleven years old at the time. It was a big life change for us. My dad had been doing construction work, so he'd leave early in the morning, he'd come home at four or five at night, and we'd all have dinner together. Obviously when the restaurant opened in '96, our lives changed drastically to the hours of restaurant people. But it's been fun so far.

What did you enjoy growing up around the business?

What I loved about it was the interacting with people constantly. It was always exciting, always changing. That is what excited me — seeing the different dynamics of not only your employees but your customers and being so involved in so many other people's lives. That was a big change for our family, obviously. Most people don't get to be in as many relationships as we're given the opportunity to be in because of the restaurant business. That was the exciting thing. Especially when you give people good food, they seem to enjoy themselves and it's usually a pleasant interaction. But even when things don't go as planned, you have an opportunity to get to know people even on a closer level by *how you handle that*. That's what intrigued me about the restaurant business.

What I didn't like was the amount of attention that it takes and the hours. It does get hard when you're working when everyone else has off. The big holidays are busy times for a restaurant. But I think that it's all relative. Every career has ups and downs. I would rather be working on a Saturday night, hanging out with our employees and our customers than sitting at home watching TV.

People often tell me, "Man, you really work a lot. You're always here." But because we did start it when I was so young, it has become a way of life for me. So, I caution people the same way. When friends are thinking about it, I always caution them and make them think about that too. For me it's easy, because it has become what we do. For some people, it is hard. It is totally different, especially when you have a family and they're at home at night and you're working. That's a whole new dynamic and I think it's important to have the support from your family because it does get challenging at times.

Even with your many years of experience, it's clear from our previous conversations you are still constantly trying to learn more about the business.

I think in this business, you constantly want to be growing and doing better because it's constantly changing. The way people are eating and what they're eating and what they expect out of food and the dining experience is always changing. That's one of the exciting things about this business — *you can't stay the same*.

There are traditions, especially with Italian food, that are never going to change. And there's one way to treat people and that's the right way. So, from the service standpoint, I don't think anyone's going to ignore good service or not appreciate that. I think those will always stay there. But the different menu items, different toppings — all those types of things are always changing. And it is fun. It's fun to experiment. Just things like arugula or Portobello mushrooms — fifteen years ago I don't think anyone cared if that was on their pizza. Now we see those types of toppings being used so much more.

The cool thing about Wisconsin — some may call it a negative but I think it's cool — is we're usually pretty far behind the trends. If something's been working for someone out in California, it usually becomes popular in Wisconsin two years later. We can piggy-back on a lot of that.

You have three locations, all in different towns…

They are. Probably around a forty-five mile radius. So, relatively close.

We just had one location until I graduated college. I guess I was probably more the motivation behind growing when I graduated. At that point we opened our second location. Then I think it was only three years after that we opened our third.

How do you find that balance of knowing when it's time to go for the next location?

I think we definitely grew too fast, although business has been good. I think it's been probably more stressful on us than it needs to be. If I could go back I would probably make sure that our systems were a lot stronger, and our processes were a lot stronger.

What's an example?

It can be anything, like even lasagna recipes. It sounds simple, but if you don't have a lasagna recipe system in place for making it the right way every time, it's amazing how your employees can start to sway from how you originally intended it to be made. Recipes can kind of get altered pretty quickly. Handling guest complaints is another. There's just an array of all aspects of the restaurant that you need to have a clear, clear way of how we do it — the rules of this restaurant. I don't know if it's intentional. Sometimes it might be, sometimes it's not. Some of your employees might start doing it this way, or say, "We'll try this, this time." That's kind of what I mean by systems and processes.

We've been able to make it work because I have my siblings involved. We're very hands-on at all of the stores. But I think for an operator that owns one restaurant and you're looking to expand, and you don't have the family help, the people that you can trust, that care as much as you do, I think those systems and processes are crucial and will go a long way.

Is it hard as you grow to let go of things and trust other people to do them?

It's very hard. I think it depends on the type of person you are. Most entrepreneurs are the type of people that know that they can *do it better themselves*. I think that's why they become entrepreneurs in the first place. They see a problem and they say, "I can do that better."

I have a good balance with my family. My dad has a little bit of that in him, obviously, whereas I'm probably a little more willing to let other people do some things. But I still think it goes back to those systems. If you can establish, "This is how we do it — this is how I know works the best," then you give that to your people and then you're *managing that system* and you're not managing those people.

I think that's where a lot of people get in trouble. You can have conversations with people and you assume that it's common sense to you, but it might not be common sense for that person because we all have different life experiences. That's why I'm just real big on getting those systems established so that everyone can agree that this is how we do it. It's not left up to your manager's perspective on things. It's not that you don't want their opinion or their perspective, because I think that's always good and that can help. But I think at that point if you decide one of your staff has a good opinion on a way to make something better, you obviously take that and then you make that the new way of doing it.

What is your long-term vision for the business?

I don't know if we have any expectations. We definitely want to grow, because there's opportunity. We all like that challenge. It's super exciting opening up stores in new markets and becoming part of new communities. That's definitely something that we're going to want to do. One thing that we're working on making sure that those systems and processes are in place so that if we do expand, it happens the right way. We're all on the same page there with my family.

Because our locations are so close, one thing that's kind of crucial is the brand identity. We've been able to carry over strong brand identity from our one store to our second to our third. It wasn't as hard as I thought it would be. I was actually pretty surprised at how much support we've had in the new communities right away. What my dad established from the get-go is how you treat people. If you look at how you do business with your employees and with your customers, it really comes down to how you're making them feel in the transaction. That to me is easy for people to see.

Pizza is pizza. You can have a better quality pizza, but that can always be duplicated. Someone can copy the way we make pizzas or somebody can copy the way we make pasta. People can copy the way we decorate or the music we play. The thing that's hard to duplicate is *how you make people feel*. That's something my parents established right away. We talk about that a lot. And that's one of the big challenges. How do you get everyone to start thinking that way? When my dad started, it was him doing it. It was him staying open a little later if a table came in at closing time and they wanted to eat. It was him that would leave the ovens on. It was him that would walk our wait staff girls out to their car at night just so they felt comfortable walking to the back alley. Little things like that I think he did probably without him even really knowing he was doing it, really showed people that he cares about them on a personal level.

How do you teach that mentality?

It is definitely hard. I think people that have been successful spend a lot of time at that part of it. Culver's is a popular burger franchise in Wisconsin here that's growing throughout the country. I know they put a lot of emphasis in the people they let run one of their franchises. Chick-fil-A is another example. They don't let just anyone run a Chick-fil-A.

I think that is crucial. You have to find people that have a natural heart for serving other people and a natural heart for wanting to make people feel a certain way. There are so many things that happen throughout the course of the day in the restaurant business. If you don't have that right mindset, then every situation is going to be different. It really comes down to who's the leader in your restaurant, and how are they going to handle those situations the right way. I think a lot of people would agree that is the challenge with growing. The people that are successful, they find good ways to train and educate so that they're always teaching that philosophy.

You own two locations and you're leasing one. Tell me about the differences. And what do you think you'll do going forward?

If you are going into locations that you might be unsure of but you have a gut feeling it might work, you could lease for a couple of years with the option to buy. That's what we did with one of our stores and it was great. It gave us a lot of security going in to say, "Well, let's see how it works for a couple years. Let's see what business is like." Really, I don't think you ever do know. You always have a good idea, but you could open a store in a location that wasn't busy before you got there and you could realize, "Holy cow, that's why this place isn't busy." The lease-to-own is always a nice option because it gives a lot of security. From a funding standpoint, a bank loves to see that you have a successful business for a couple years before they're going to give you a lot of money.

The store that we leased, it's been nice to have a little less worries and a little less upkeep as far as you have someone plowing your driveway and stuff like that for you. But I think the smarter business move is always try to *own the dirt* that you're doing business on. Owning from a business standpoint is always better. But from a security standpoint, being able to lease and not having that huge commitment is always a good option too, maybe even just to get started.

What advice do you have about lease agreements?

The big thing with lease negotiations is that they're negotiable. One thing I learned from my dad is that everything's negotiable. Don't just look at the lease and say, "Okay, that's what I'm going to pay. That's what I'm going to do." Really try and make it what's good for your business going into it, because the last thing anyone wants is for you to get into something that's not good and you are not able to make it work.

In our one location, signage has been an issue. It's something that you can overlook in the whole process. It's something I overlooked. It's the lack of good signage from the road and that's kind of been a struggle. Consider who pays for what in a lease agreement. If the furnace goes out on the top of the roof, who's going to pay to fix that? Once you get into it, you really understand the importance of that kind of stuff. You want to be thorough and ask the dumb questions if you have to so that you understand.

How do you find the balance between looking forward to new locations, but also paying attention to your existing locations?

Our philosophy is that we want to be a blessing to other people and we actually do care about how you feel. I don't think we ever take that for granted. I think as long as your philosophy is right and you keep that on the forefront of why you're doing what you're doing, that's important. If I get complaints from our first store I'm not going to take that for granted just because it's been there or just because they've had our great established business there. I think it comes down to truly caring about the people. That's our philosophy. It's just who we are. I think we care equally about all those things, so that's how we've dealt with that.

But it is hard. It'll be interesting to see how the future goes because it's hard to let go. One of the things that is hard to let go of is those relationships that you create with your employees and customers. Making sure that those things stay intact is a challenge. At the same time, you do want to grow and you want to do better. I guess we're going to have to see how that goes. If we can keep our mindset right on why we're doing what we're doing, I think we can manage that whole process the right way.

How do spread the word about Christianos?

I think the most effective way is word-of-mouth. It's spending time with the customers you do have and making sure that their experience is good. It's amazing when you get to a different level with your customers as far as more of an emotional experience than just a food experience.

Everyone says that it's the best form of marketing. But, no one really tells you how to do it. For us it's been creating those relationships with people on a more personal level and showing them that we do care genuinely about them as people through their dining experience. It can be just showing them that you care when an order gets screwed up, or making sure that they have a condiment they need, just any little thing in recognizing people's needs. I've personally seen how that just changes people's impression of you and your business. It's amazing how you can go from just being another restaurant to being *the greatest* restaurant of all time when people have those experiences in your store.

Other than that, we'll do some events with the community. Fundraisers are good for everybody. If you can help a local charity raise some money and draw people into your store to help raise money for that, that's probably one of the best ways. Maybe not even so much for getting new people in your store on that specific day. But it goes towards creating the relationship with the people that are with that organization, and showing them that you care, that you're going to maybe give ten percent of your profits that night to a certain charity. That really means a lot to the people that are running these local organizations. Then they obviously go and talk about that.

That's what makes this business exciting. If you can teach your employees to look for those opportunities, to go to that next level and show people that you care about them, it makes you as a person feel good doing it for them. It's something we talk about a lot with our employees. It's harder for some people than others. A lot of people, they still don't get it. It's a funny joke that we have. I just had a conversation with some of our staff the other day. I'm like, "You can give away whatever you want if you need to make someone happy. I'll yell at you after the fact." (Laughs) You have the freedom and confidence to do whatever you think you need to do to make sure that that person understands that we care about them. It's not a natural thing for a lot of people. To get people to think outside the box, to go that extra mile for people, it's interesting and challenging. But when you see it happen, it's a good feeling for everybody.

Treat other people how you'd want to be treated. It really is a simple but profound business philosophy that works every time. It requires reminding people, "Would you really want to be treated like that?" It's a simple concept that is very overlooked, especially in today's society.

Are there any books that you would recommend for people getting into the restaurant business?

Setting the Table by Danny Meyer is an awesome book, and is helpful not only for the restaurant business but for business in general. And speaking of Chick-fil-A, Truett Cathy (Chick-fil-A's founder) has written a lot of books. Any book that he's written has been really good.

Start with Why by Simon Sinek goes along with that same philosophy of why do you do what you do. Everyone knows what they do, but not always why. He uses a lot of examples of the companies that really understand their why, and it's clear that they're running a superior business to the companies that don't understand their why.

Jess Kileen

Grassburger

TWO LOCATIONS - DURGANGO, CO AND
ALBUQUERQUE, NM

RESTAURANT OWNER SINCE 2014

Tell me the story of Grassburger and what prompted you and Ed to get started in this business.

Well, it actually has everything to do with family. Two of our three boys have severe food allergies. Going out to eat became an enormous challenge. Whether we were traveling or even in our hometown, we had our designated places, but it always seemed to come down to burgers. That was the safe food, for the most part, and the boys loved hamburgers. So, I started really looking at diet and nutrition and the differences in burgers and meats and what have you. Grass-fed beef kept coming up — not just grass-fed beef, but other livestock and cage-free eggs as well. Animals that are raised this way changes the composition of the meat and it's much better for the creatures and for human consumption. As a result of what we were learning, we went exclusively to grass-fed beef at home. We even started having burger parties at our house and people were, like, "Boy, this meat is so delicious!" That evolved to, "If we're going to go out for a burger, wouldn't it be great if we could find a grass-fed burger?" Once we started looking, it was very difficult to find. Or if we found it, it was twenty dollars for the burger.

That wasn't a sustainable price model for us to go out to eat. We're a family of five. So, one day Ed and I sat down and wrote the entire manifesto for Grassburger. What we would want it to look like? How could it be allergy-friendly? How could it be the most nutrition for the least amount of money, trying to keep it really pocketbook friendly? It fell right into that fast-casual restaurant model that's become more and more popular.

Had you been in the restaurant business prior to this?

Absolutely not. I wanted to have a ranch and raise grass-fed beef, but Ed grew up on a farm and he was opposed. He said, "I'm not spending my weekends working." Of course, we opened a restaurant and that's all we do on the weekends, so I don't know if we've succeeded in that arena. But I think we did succeed in creating a burger model that is a healthier, more sustainable and price-conscious. In the lab, if you take a sampling of grass-fed versus grain-fed beef, the scientific difference between them is astounding. Grass-fed beef is higher in good fats (Omega 3s) and lower in bad fats, lower in calories, and higher in amino acids and vitamins such as CLAs (conjugated linoleic acid), Vitamin A, E, etc.

Tell me about corn-fed beef, which is commonly used for burgers.

Corn has become, in the United States at least, a relatively common staple to help fatten up beef and get them ready for slaughter sooner. It's become part of the whole economic model for the beef industry. For ranchers that have switched over to grass-fed, it requires a longer incubation period. Their business model shifts. It's a significant thing from a rancher's perspective to make that changeover.

Our supplier is the Rain Crow Ranch out of Missouri. They're four thousand acres, nineteen hundred heads of cattle. They converted to exclusively grass-fed primarily because Patricia (Patricia and Mark run it) is a large animal vet. She started seeing a lot of health issues in the animals she was treating. She was able to connect that directly to what they were eating. Once they switched all their animals over to grass-fed exclusively, those issues just went away.

Because grass is what they're meant to eat...

That's what they're meant to eat — exactly! When they're on things that their bodies aren't designed to eat, they end up with digestive issues and infections. It makes them much more susceptible. As the consumer, when we're eating grass-fed it's just a cleaner, more digestible meat for us as well. You don't have the heavy impact of antibiotics and hormones that come with it.

I've heard you can fatten the cattle with corn the last two months of their lives and still technically say they were "grass fed."

There are a lot of ways you can raise your cattle. We are committed to one hundred percent grass-fed. The research shows that if you have cattle that's grass-fed, and you take them off of it and put them on corn or put them in a feedlot, the benefits of grass-fed decrease by the day that they are off of the grass. We've made a commitment to keep our beef supply one hundred percent grass-fed.

When did you start Grassburger?

We opened the Durango store two years ago, July of 2014. We opened the second one in Albuquerque, in the Northeast Heights area, in March of this year (2016). It's a beautiful store. It's so fun to having a restaurant that's brand new. Everything's still shiny and clean.

How long did you plan before you opened your first location?

It took us about a year to lead up to writing the business plan and then about six months to get the financing and plans in place. Albuquerque was much faster. That was super speed.

Do you think you benefitted in some ways during planning by not having prior experience in the business?

Probably beneficial and detrimental, all wrapped up on one pretty package. Ignorance is bliss. I think that having a fresh perspective has been great. But, boy, our *learning curve was so big*, in terms of equipment and ordering and inventory and the actual mechanics of running a business. Initially we hired on a restaurant consultant. He was really helpful because we didn't know anything about the equipment and how to make an ordering list, etc. We hired good people — that makes all the difference in the world. We have a great team and staff and managers. We learned from them. And we continue to learn and pivot as needed.

We've certainly had our share of mistakes in terms of hiring. The restaurant industry is volatile and hard for employees and employers. You have a lot of turnover. Durango is challenging because a lot of the staff that work in the restaurants here are in college. They're looking for part time work, and while they're motivated because they want to pay their rent, they also all have break at the same time — they tend to go away for the summer. So, you have these distinctive hiring times. There are times when you go from one hundred percent coverage of your shifts to all of sudden you have twenty-five percent coverage, and nobody's available.

How long were you open when you decided to open another location in Albuquerque?

About six months. Ed was talking about it very, very quickly. His background is commercial development. When we were writing the business plan for Grassburger, in our minds we had a model that would be replicable. We tried to create systems that would be able to be *reproduced easily*. We consider Durango our flagship, and Albuquerque is a foray into what that looks like on a larger scale. It's been very interesting having this sister store. In very short order, it has showed us where we have work to do, and where we succeeded.

What is an example of something you realized you need to work on?

Our employee training program. We were still really evolving that in Durango when we opened up Albuquerque. And then suddenly Albuquerque was ramping up and we had three different managers, two in Durango and one in Albuquerque, and they had really different management styles. We were trying to finalize a training system in Durango and in the meantime the Albuquerque store staff is getting trained in a different way out of necessity. We had to pull that back, quickly finalize our process in Durango, and then implement that in Albuquerque.

How far is Albuquerque from Durango?

Three-and-a-half hours.

Why did you choose Albuquerque?

Part of it is drive time. It's really close compared to a Denver or Colorado Springs or some of the other larger metropolis areas. You can be back and forth in a day if you have to.

But we really like Albuquerque, more than anything. It has a strong but fresh farm-to-table, we call it "farm-to-families," movement. There are some interesting demographics in terms of people's awareness of food, and what they're eating. I was really intrigued by being at the forefront of that, whereas in some of these other cities that is so established and our concept is really old news.

What do you offer other than grass-fed beef?

Our menu was very, very simple. But we've added Applegate chicken hot dogs, which are all natural — no nitrates or fillers. We just added taco plates, green chile beef and vegan black bean/quinoa. We also do a vegan black bean quinoa burger, which we make in-house. And we make all of our salad dressings and chipotle mayo from scratch. The reason we do that is because then we can make foods that have no corn syrup, no fillers. It's all one hundred percent olive oil and good mustard and apple cider vinegar, cage-free eggs — high quality ingredients, the way we cook at home.

We also serve hand-cut French fries and sweet potato fries. We keep our fryers dedicated to those items. We don't allow any other food items because we're trying to keep them gluten free, and also make sure that they're not contaminated with any dairy products or any nut products.

We're avoiding cross contamination wherever we can to keep it simple for people who have allergies. It's difficult to go into a restaurant with a food allergy and figure out *what's safe and what isn't*. The same is true if you are avoiding gluten or eat paleo or whatever you may have in terms of dietary restrictions. Our menu is designed to make that process simple for users.

We source our greens from local farmers. We get as many parts of our salad from local producers as we can. We can't do that all year - in our climate, when we start to get into winter I have to buy organic produce through our vendors. But as long as there's someone growing in the area, we're interested in supporting them. We have a backdoor farmers' market going on.

Was it difficult to find vendors and processes to use clean local produce?

Yes and no. It's difficult from a cost standpoint. By purchasing vegetables from the farmers' market versus from the grocery you pay more. Yes, you are supporting those farmers and that local piece, and that's so important. But there is that step up in cost. When you're building a restaurant model, cost is a huge part of whatever your margins are. The way we have worked it out with our salad piece is that we blend our margin. We know that local organic produce isn't available all year-round so we do a blended back margin in our books. The months of the year we're buying from vendors have a significant decrease in cost - and then that enables us to pay more in the seasons that it's available.

Is your consumer base educated about what you are doing?

It depends. Durango is a foodie town. We have more restaurants per capita here than San Francisco. But Albuquerque is a much bigger melting pot. One of the issues that came up in Albuquerque is the value of our pricing. People are used to going to a place like Freddy's which is a local burger/shake place that's really a step above McDonalds in terms of pricing. You get this massive amount of meat. People who don't know or never heard of grass-fed beef are going, "Well, why am I paying this for this when I can go over here and get that?" We're really having to address the *why* of grass-fed beef — all the pieces that make it special, better for the animals, better for our bodies, better for the planet.

The other thing that has come up for us is the size of our patty, because we serve a quarter pound patty. That's part of our ethos. According to the

USDA, four to nine ounces of meat is what a person should be eating in a day for protein. So, four ounces is a healthy and appropriate portion. We offer a quarter pound and a half pound patty. We're really trying to wrap in this idea of, "Okay, this is an appropriate, healthy and satisfying amount of meat."

What does the future hold for Grassburger?

We're still stabilizing Albuquerque. We'll see what happens. If you were to talk to Ed, he would say "Let's start looking around and finding our next spot." I'm the one that's going, "Hold on, hold on." We have that dynamic.

What's been the most satisfying part of Grassburger?

On a personal note, I love feeding people. I love cooking and making meals, so the best part for me is being out on the floor of the restaurant and talking to people who are eating. We get a lot of positive feedback about the taste of the meat. We won the Durango Herald's Reader's Choice Award for "Best Burger and Fries" last summer. We weren't even a year open. That was a huge deal, because the burger designation in this town is fiercely competitive and we won it by a landslide. I have a lot of pride around that because we were so new. *But it wasn't about me — it was about the meat.* Talking to people and seeing their faces when they take that first bite. It never gets old.

On the flip side of that, what's been the biggest challenge you've had to overcome?

The biggest challenges are really more about just simply business things. Learning this industry, staffing and training and consistency and communication — all those parts. I feel like we're really solid on our intent and on our product but the everyday restaurant things that come up are always surprising.

Is there anything you want to share with your peers in the industry and folks that want to get into the restaurant business?

I do have to give Schedulefly a plug. Using Schedulefly has been one of the decisions that has made running our business so much easier. We *love* your product. All the employees can access it all the time. We're able to give messages to staff about things that come up at once. And we just started using the posting capability. We just revised our manual and put it up on

Schedulefly for the staff to access. It's been a great tool. I'm thrilled about it!

I wasn't expecting you to say that. Thank you.

I meant it.

Pies & Pints

TWELVE LOCATIONS IN BIRMINGHAM AND
MONTGOMERY, AL, COLUMBUS, WORTHINGTON,
DAYTON AND CINCINNATI, OH, CHARLESTON,
MORGANTOWN AND FAYETTEVILLE, WV,
LEXINGTON KY

RESTAURANT OWNER SINCE 2003

How did you get started in the restaurant industry?

My degree is in business — marketing and management — but from the time I was 15-years-old I was working in restaurants. I started out washing dishes at a small mom and pop neighborhood place. When I turned 16 I got a job in a fast food restaurant, and after that I went to a casual dining pizza restaurant where I bussed tables, served, delivered pizza and cooked. I just stayed in the industry and worked my way up through fine dining, bartending, banquet serving — I did it all.

I had a restaurant before I started Pies & Pints. I had a coffee shop café for about three years, but I realized I wasn't a morning person so I sold it and traveled for a bit. A friend of mine was the food and beverage director at a ski resort in Utah and she asked me to come out and work with her, so I did.

Is that where your partnership began?

That's where I met David, who was from New York. He grew up working in his dad's pizza shop in Long Island. I was the manager and he was the assistant manager of an intimate fine dining restaurant at the resort. We had a similar work ethic and we worked well together. I started telling him how I thought a pizza place would do well in Fayetteville. He eventually said, "Alright, let's do it." So, we went back to Fayetteville and I borrowed about twenty thousand dollars on a credit card and we started in the basement of an old house.

Four years later we expanded to a new location three times the size. Now we're getting ready to open our ninth location.

With your coffee shop, you were on your own for three years. What made you decide to work with a partner this time?

I learned a lot of lessons owning that restaurant. I learned I wasn't a morning person and I learned that I needed a business partner, someone to share the highs and the lows with. Because when you're low, being low alone is not that fun. And when you're high, being high alone — that doesn't really sound that great but you know what I'm trying to say. A good business partner's weaknesses are your strengths and vice versa. David and I made a good team because most of his experience was back of the house and most of my experience was front of the house.

Credit card debt and a basement. I love that!

We had between us maybe five thousand dollars. We had the credit card. Back then, in 2003, you could have a Visa with really low interest. I was able to get twenty thousand dollars and I think the first year was maybe zero percent and then it went to seven percent or something. Basically, we just used a credit card to get started. And then once we were up and running I took all of that debt to a banker and consolidated it. We got an SBA loan, I think It was a seven-year loan for around forty thousand dollars at 11% interest.

This space had already been used for a sub shop, so it had some tables, chairs and refrigeration. We bought all used equipment and Dave and I did all of the demolition ourselves. We got one person to help us with building everything out. We had maybe twenty seats inside and about thirty seats outside. We got open that year in April and we were closed by the end of October. That first year we were only open for those months and then David and I had to go get jobs. We reopened again in March the next year, so those first two years we were actually seasonal.

You focused on the quality of your food – instead of using sugar, you use honey, and you use filtered water instead of regular water, and kosher salt instead regular salt. How do you think this emphasis on quality contributed to your success?

In 2003 in Fayetteville, a rural town in West Virginia, our pizza was different than the pizza that they were used to. In other parts of the country this was nothing new. Everybody was doing high quality stuff back then. The other thing that was new for this area at that time was that we were only doing craft beer. In fact when we first opened, we tried to do no Budweiser. Two things we were adamant amount were no Bud, and no ranch dressing. We eventually caved to the Bud, but only in bottles, never on tap. All of our tap handles, except 1 for PBR, are reserved for craft beer.

But we still, to this day, have no ranch dressing. That's something we're very proud of. I joke around about writing a book called The Ranchification of America, because I feel like ever since ranch dressing was invented people don't have to have food that tastes good, they can just have anything and dip it in ranch. Our point was our pizza is good enough that you don't have to dip it in ranch. You can eat the crust and it has flavor and it tastes good. It stands on its own. I would educate the staff so they could explain when people would ask why we don't have ranch dressing.

We do make our own creamy gorgonzola so if people really insist on having something to dip their crust in, we suggest the creamy gorgonzola.

So you needed to educate your customer base…

Yeah, we opened that first restaurant in a rural town in West Virginia. It's a huge tourist town, lots of rock climbers and rafters who come from Washington, D.C., Charlotte, NC, Richmond VA and various other cities. The tourists kind of got what we were doing. But as far as the locals … yes, we spent a lot of time on education. Educating our staff to educate the customers on why we were doing what we were doing. We wanted them to experience something they had never experienced before.

We would educate the servers to understand that if a guest said, "I only drink Budweiser," they could recommend other lagers. Maybe not every single person would change, but one out of five would at least taste it and then they would consider it. People would tell us, "I never thought I'd like any other beer except for Bud Lite, but now I'm drinking this other local beer." Mission accomplished.

Even with our pizza we had to educate people. We put our sauce on top, not the bottom. Our cheese bakes into the crust and the sauce doesn't make it soggy. We use fresh herbs instead of dried. We put grapes on a pizza — people had never heard of that. All of that stuff made us stand out, made us be different. *It started a conversation*. People said, "Oh, you have to try this pizza place. They put grapes on the pizza. I know it's crazy but, you're going to love it." We tried to raise the bar on everything we did and *we tried not to do what everyone else was doing*. Back then barbeque chicken pizza was popular so we did a chipotle chicken pizza instead. Now chipotle is pretty common.

Dave and I really like food. We had this Cuban pork sandwich with pulled pork in Colorado somewhere, and we thought, "This would be awesome on a pizza." And that's one of my favorite pizzas. We roast our own pork butts in house. And then the pizza – pork, pineapple, jalapenos, cilantro – it's just full of flavor. We finish it with crème fraiche, and it's really good.

Did you have doubts during the first year or two?

In the early years, the off seasons were hard for sure. It was in the basement of a house and it was really drafty and old and cold. We only had a few seats inside and even then, sometimes we still couldn't fill them. People were still getting used to this idea of even just knowing that we're there and that we're open in the winter time. We had to rely on just the locals and it was hard.

We learned that consistency was key. You have to be open. ***You have to stick to your hours no matter what***. You can't close at seven o'clock because nobody's in the restaurant. If you say you're going to be open until eight or nine o'clock, then you have to stay open until eight or nine o'clock. We stuck to it. It's kind of industry standard that January and February are your slowest months, but we are finally making money during the off season. It took a long time.

When we first opened I thought we might just be a seasonal restaurant, but the fact that we stay open and are even profitable in those months says to me that you can educate. We have diehard people, locals, that love our restaurant. Just sticking to your plan and knowing as long as you see a couple more people every time and you have people that tell you they really appreciate what you're doing. We never thought, let's cut corners and start doing what everybody else is doing. Not one time. If anything, we try to go in the opposite direction.

At times I would think that maybe we should do coal-fired or wood-fired or maybe we should try to go pizza Napoletana – only water, flour, oil. But our pizza is solid and we like our product. And when we try to change, there are issues that come about that you don't anticipate. It's easy to do wood-fired if you only have a certain amount of customers. But we get really, really busy at times. We'll do three to four hundred pizzas on a Saturday night. So, our pizza is really good and it really works for the style of pizza we're doing and the amount of volume that we're doing.

Tell me about the growth process.

2006 is when we bought a new building because we had two hour waits at the old basement location. We actually had a park that we overflowed into, so we were lucky because we could kind of serve people in the park. But in 2006 we were up to two hour waits and we were just bursting at the seams. We bought a building, moved there and went from having about 50 seats to having over a hundred seats — 60 inside and another 50 outside on a covered patio. We got that open in 2007, and immediately when we opened we already had waits again, so by the next season we added fifty more seats. So then we had around a hundred and fifty seats total — fifty of those were outside, so they were seasonal but that works for us because we're a seasonal restaurant.

So now we're in this really big space. We have a lot of room and everything's doing well and that's 2007 — that's when we reached economies of scale. Up until this point David and I, we had to be in the restaurant all the time, because we were busy but we weren't making enough money that we could actually pay managers. I think we maxed out at around four hundred thousand a year gross sales at the original location, and then in 2007 when we went to the new location we jumped up to almost eight hundred thousand that year. So then we could afford to pay some managers.

A lot of people had asked us, "Can you open one here? Open one there?" We started talking, and thought maybe we should do another location. We started looking at some places within an hour to two hours of our original location. The closest next big town to Fayetteville is Charleston, which is the capital. We considered several other towns, but we found a really great space in Charleston. We knew we already had a good customer base there, because lots of people did the hour drive to Fayetteville. It was early in 2010 that we found that space and started working on it. We opened in December of that year.

How different was opening a second location compared to your first experience?

It was actually really hard getting that restaurant open. David opened another restaurant that same year. He and his wife (she was his fiancé at the time) have a concept they started in Fayetteville called the Secret Sandwich Society. So David was kind of working on that. I ended up opening the Charleston store on my own. David helped when he could but not as much as he had helped in the past. It kind of wore on our relationship, a lot of arguments and a lot of stress. But we got it up and running and it was very, very successful right out of the gate. When we first opened, right around Christmas time, we were doing eight to ten thousand dollars a day, every day.

We had that open for a few months and I think it was around March that some people approached us and said they liked our concept and they wanted to know what our growth plan was. David and I had already decided that we were not going to do anymore restaurants. We were happy with the two and that was plenty for us.

But then the two gentlemen approached us and we all came to an agreement where we were going to form a new company and the Charleston store would be the first store of the new company. They weren't interested in the Fayetteville store because it was too seasonal and not really a concept store. David and I took a smaller piece of a bigger pie. We kind of stepped back. I still do marketing for the company. David is working on his other business, so he doesn't have any sort of management in the new company. Rob Lindeman, who used to be the president/CEO of another restaurant, became our CEO and president and he is the one that has grown the company from two stores to nine locations, with more to come. He finds the locations, negotiates the leases and gets the restaurants open. The only franchise we have as of right now is the Morgantown store. All the other locations are company owned with some outside investment. We sell shares in each of the restaurants. We own seventy percent and thirty percent is private investors.

Congratulations on the growth. That's a big change! Was that a hard transition to make?

I don't think it was for David at all. For me, I was really excited about doing it just because getting that second location was so stressful that it was kind of nice to think about handing it over to somebody else to do all the hard work. But then part of me was like, "What am I doing?" Lots of people told me it would be hard for me to give up control. The first location Rob opened was in Worthington, OH which is close to where he lives. David and I didn't see it the new space much until the soft opening. We had mixed reactions to the store, but the food was spot on, so that was very positive. When we originally met with our new partners, they asked us, "What are your sacred cows? What are the things that you're not willing to give up on, you're not willing to sacrifice?" David and I came up with some things and told them.

No ranch dressing!

That was exactly one of them — no ranch dressing. One thing we forgot about was that we never wanted to have TVs in our restaurant. Our first restaurant didn't have any TVs, and in the second restaurant, we kind of caved and we had two TVs. The new location had eight TVs. We were like, "Oh, my God, we forgot about the TVs." It just had this totally different feel that we just didn't think about. We were always very specific about what we put on the TVs. If there wasn't a major sporting event on we always had it on Fuel TV. I don't even know if it that channel still exists, but it always had snowboarding or surfing or what we thought were cool and kind of extreme sports. That's the vibe we wanted for the restaurant. That's what we thought of when we thought of Pies & Pints, because our original location was in Fayetteville which is a rock-climbing-white-water-kayaking-mountain biking, kind of an extreme sports town. We wanted it to fit that feel.

We didn't think about how the extreme sport feel translated into an Ohio suburban restaurant. We walk in and not only are there eight TVs, I think The Shark Tank was on one of them. David and I were aghast, but we sat down and we talked to Rob and we told him how we felt. There were some other things that weren't as big as the TVs, but TV thing is the one thing that stood out in my mind. We sat down and we discussed that this isn't what we expected.

Was that difficult?

That first meeting felt like it was us against him. I think he felt that way too, thinking, "I didn't sign on for this. I don't want to be challenged on every decision I make." We had that one meeting and we all walked away from it and thought about what each other said and from then on, it's really been kind of smooth sailing. Does he do everything the way that David and I would do it? No. But, David and I learned to kind of accept the fact that we're not in charge anymore and we enjoy the freedom we have from this new arrangement.

We like that we have the nine restaurants and we don't even have to set foot in these restaurants. They just open and we go to the opening parties and taste the food and make sure it tastes just like the recipes we gave them the day we signed the deal. I'm not saying that everybody's going to be that lucky to have everything go that smoothly. But the deal that we have struck, the direction we took, we're ninety-nine percent pleased.

Has your philosophy about running a restaurant changed from when you started to now?

I recently had a baby so that has made me very aware of what it is like to dine out with a kid. Most people in the restaurant industry are young and don't have kids, so they are not that psyched to wait on kids. If you don't have kids, and you see a bunch kids come in the restaurant, you're thinking, man, they're going to make a mess. It's not a server's favorite thing. But you have to cater to kids. If you can win the kids over, ***then you've got the parents as loyal customers***. In Fayetteville, we actually have a playground outside in the back of the restaurant. It's cute. Parents tell me all the time that if they're going to go out to eat, they need to be able to go somewhere that the kids can go. I'm not saying you have to build a playground. But you need to think of things for the kids and keep the kids in mind. Teach your staff that the kids are the most important thing. Because to the parents, they're the most important thing.

Also, I spend a lot of time out in Portland, and there are a lot of chef-owned or chef-driven restaurants which are great. Lots of times restaurants like this won't let you make substitutions or changes to the dishes, which I totally appreciate and understand, but not everyone does. We make a real effort to never say "No." For example, if someone wants ranch dressing we say, "We don't have ranch dressing, but we do have creamy gorgonzola if you would like to try that." I tell my staff to *figure out a way to say "Yes"* to people. Don't say "No" and leave it at that. You've got to turn it around and make it a positive thing. Sometimes people take too much pride in saying, "Well, we don't do that." I think that it's just offensive to people. People don't want to hear "No." If you can't figure out a way to say "Yes" then you're in the wrong business.

One of the other big things we do at Pies & Pints is that while our hours on the door say we close at ten o'clock, if somebody walks in at ten-oh-five or ten-ten, ten-fifteen and see people in the restaurant and the ovens are still on, we do not turn them away. That's another thing I cannot stand is when you go to a restaurant and somebody got seated two minutes before you did, and you walk in and they'll just say, "Sorry, we're closed." Really? Not, "Can we get you something to go?" But as a server, when I was young I was guilty of saying, "Sorry, we're closed" because nobody ever trained me otherwise.

When we interview people, we let them know right away that this is how we run our business. Yeah, the hours on the door say ten o'clock, but that doesn't mean we close at ten o'clock. You need to be prepared. And if you prepare people and you educate the staff and they know that, then they don't get pissed off. They just know that's part of their job, that's how we run this business.

If I had to say one word that is a theme in our restaurant and has made our business successful, it's education. Educating staff. Educating the customers. Everybody knows what's going on, what you're trying to do, what your goal is, what you're trying to accomplish.

Five Bar

SIX LOCATIONS - BIRMINGHAM, MOBILE AND TUSCALOOSA, AL, ATHENS, GA AND KNOXVILLE AND CHATTANOOGA, TN

Chuck's Fish

THREE LOCATIONS – BIRMINGHAM, MOBILE AND TUSCALOOSA, AL

RESTAURANT OWNER SINCE 2005

How did you get started in the restaurant industry?

I was born and raised in Tokyo. My mother is Japanese and our family has had successful restaurants in the Tokyo area for several generations. I grew up in the business and when I was twelve years old moved to the United States. After high school I got a degree from the University of West Florida. I worked in Boston as a software developer for about three years, all the while knowing that eventually I was going to be in the restaurant business.

My mother had partnered with Charles Morgan, who is the owner of Harbor Docks down in Destin. She put our family sushi bars into his concepts. Charles had known me since I was a young teenager, and when I got back home to Destin, FL in 2002, I started managing his restaurant.

Three years later I was partnered in by Charles and opened my first restaurant, called Camille's. And now eleven years later, my business partner is still Charles and we opened all of the Chuck's Fish and the FIVE restaurants together.

You have a unique concept with "FIVE", standing for the number five in your menu categories (five appetizers, five beers, etc.) How did you develop this concept?

It's based on the premise that while there are obviously many wonderful restaurants out there, there's a lot of them that we feel can be overwhelming in regards to the menu. *We wanted a restaurant that's based on the concept of doing a few things but doing those things really well.*

I found that even with this simple style of the menu, our guests seem to still have a difficult time deciding what to order. We understand that if you only have five entrees they better be pretty dang good. Expectations are raised tremendously when somebody walks in our door. And so, while expectations are high, the simplicity of the menu also gives us a chance to really focus on what we're doing.

Does that mean your operations are simpler than most restaurants' operations?

Well, there's something to be said for keeping things simple, but I shouldn't give anybody the impression that having a simple menu means these operations are simple to run. It just really puts more pressure on you. If there are only five things on the menu, your staff members need to know every single intricate detail about everything that's on it.

The thing about the five that we offer, it's honest food. We don't cut any corners. And we stay away from trends.

I am younger than my partner and I tend to be attracted to trends more than he is. It's a struggle for him to try to keep me focused on staying simple with the concept. *It takes discipline to stay simple*. I'm incredibly fortunate that my partner Charles is also my mentor. He constantly preaches to stay focused on what we do, and not fall into the trends when people say "You need to put this or that on your menu." We stick with what we're doing and hopefully it'll continue to be a success.

In 2014 you raised your minimum wage for your non-tipped employees. Why was that important?

We did it before it became a national issue. We are only as good as the people that work alongside us. That's why it is so important to keep employees happy. We have staff, especially in the kitchen, that quite frankly work their butts off every single night in working conditions that aren't that glamorous. We call them porters - we don't call them dishwashers - because they do a little bit of everything and they're in the back getting after it. When it comes down to it, we want our porters to be able to make enough money to afford to eat in the restaurant that they work in. So, we raised the minimum wage in all of our stores across the board to ensure that we're providing a decent wage for the people that are working incredibly hard for us.

Why don't you do traditional advertising?

Let me preface by saying that we support advertisers. We think it's a wonderful profession and career. And we're not advocates of other restaurants not advertising. It's just our personal way of doing things. There's money that is normally allocated for marketing or PR expenses, but we wanted that money to serve a purpose other than just promoting ourselves.

My partner Charles has been doing many wonderful things for many years in regards to raising money for the less fortunate. Once a year he raises money and takes hundreds of kids fishing - he's been doing this for over twenty years. He buys them their own rods and reels, gathers a bunch of charter boats that come together, and takes kids out fishing that normally don't get a chance to. They end the big day with a fish fry for all the kids. It's through the different avenues like that where we like to allocate a lot of our marketing expense — *if you're going to spend the money, have it put to good use*.

Another example of this is that we were approached by the local YMCA to sponsor an underprivileged youth football team. At that point Charles stepped up and said, "Instead of sponsoring a team, why don't we just sponsor your entire league?" So, the several thousand dollars funded the equipment and uniforms for the entire league. In return, they put our restaurant logo on the kids' uniforms. However, instead of one team having a Chuck's Fish logo, the entire league has a Chuck's Fish logo on their jersey - just a different colored jersey for each team.

You also have a not-for-profit food truck operation...

I take great pride and interest in this operation. It was an idea that came up while Charles's son, Chatham Morgan, was taking a course at the University of Alabama, where we have two restaurants and a coffee shop. During that course, he had the idea of a nonprofit company that was mobile in nature - a food truck that is not-for-profit. It's based on the premise that while there are many soup kitchens out there doing wonderful things, a lot of times people that are in need of the services of a soup kitchen can't transport themselves to go get the food. And so, we began the operation of having a kitchen that can be transported and driven to impoverished locations to give out free lunch.

The company is called American Lunch, a 501(c)3 non-profit organization. It is operated through volunteers, most of which are employees, but we invite the community to help volunteer with the truck. We create these restaurant quality meals, like Gulf seafood gumbo, or red beans & rice with sausage. Our chefs prepare these meals and we pack the food truck up, which is then driven then to impoverished locations and give out free meals. We currently have four trucks in operation — Tuscaloosa, Athens, Knoxville, and Chattanooga.

We operate the food trucks every Monday, Wednesday, and Friday. We post to our website — americanlunch.org — the different locations and the type of foods we'll be serving every week. And people always can check in with that to see where the food truck is going to be. On average I would say we serve about 80-100 lunches a day. Since its inception in July of 2012, we're at about 30,000 lunches that we've served so far.

That's amazing! That must be very rewarding.

There's a ton of people who would not be able to eat a lunch for one reason or another. We pull the truck up into their parking lot, open the window of the food truck, and we have a line out there of people just waiting for these free meals that we give out.

It really is a wonderful thing, and not only for the people that are receiving the food. My partners and I realize that we're in a position where we employ a lot of the younger generation. We have over three hundred fifty employees amongst the eight stores, and the staff is still very impressionable. *It gives us an opportunity to teach these young minds that if you are in a position to, you should help somebody out*. We only hope to serve as an example to other people to say, listen, if you're in a good position, if you're profitable, and if you've done good for yourself, help somebody else out. There's more to this business other than trying to pad that bottom line.

We've been fortunate to be successful in the business of selling food that it's really not a big deal for us to be giving some of it away. At all of our restaurants we do a Thanksgiving Charity Feast where on Thanksgiving Day at every location our chefs prepare an incredible meal that they work on for weeks. We open all of our doors on Thanksgiving Day for the general public and anybody — no questions asked — is welcome to come into our restaurant on that day and enjoy a wonderful Thanksgiving meal. It brings in all walks of life, from people who can't afford a meal, or an affluent family that doesn't want to 'do the dishes' this year. And perhaps that family will write us a check and give it to us as a donation, because they know that we're picking a local charity to help out, that we take all the money that's been donated to us on that day and we give it all to that charity. In Knoxville last year, I believe we served close to five hundred meals on Thanksgiving Day, and we were able to raise almost four thousand dollars. We picked a local charity called The Love Kitchen, and the day after Thanksgiving we took a check for $4000 over to them. They liked that.

In situations like that we do get media attention, as to say "Hey, you guys are doing a great thing." But, honestly, the heroes in this situation are not us. It's those people over at The Love Kitchen who do this every single day of their lives.

I love the way you approach your business. Your philosophy is inspiring.

We do things unconventionally and we don't really do things the typical way. At the same time, we try to keep things as simple as possible, and try to have fun doing it.

Angela Salamanca

Centro

RALEIGH, NC

RESTAURANT OWNER SINCE 2007

Tell me about your background.

I graduated from high school in Bogota, Colombia in 1993, which seems like forever ago. I applied to college and I did not get in. Mom and Dad decided that it would be a good idea for me to come to the States and take six months before I could apply to college again. My Uncle Carlos was here and he owned a restaurant. They said, "Why don't you just go and hang out with him. You can practice your English. Then you can come back and take the test again and you can just start the rest of your life." Bogota in the late 1990's was a really difficult city to be in — very, very violent. There was a lot of stuff going on with the drug cartels. But because that's where you are, you don't question it — it's just part of your natural environment. I didn't even realize how lucky I was coming here to see Carlos for what I thought it was going to be a six-month break.

I started working with him right away. I was seventeen. I didn't stress that I was away from Mom and Dad. Especially Mom, because I grew up with a single mother and she was very involved and very controlling. Being here away from her and away from home was really interesting. It literally opened my eyes to the possibilities of what could happen for me in life. So I started working with my uncle. Carlos owns this very famous restaurant in Raleigh called Dos Taquitos. He's been open for, I think, twenty-four years. He has been the base of a lot of things that have happened with our family in terms of businesses. Carlos is a very generous, generous human being. He's always taking people in from our family to help them out, whether it's for a temporary period of time, or to start a partnership or an adventure. He's always been very generous.

I was here with another teenager that from Colombia, and we started working at Dos Taquitos. I remember the first Friday we ever worked, they sent us to run food in the kitchen. It was such chaos to see all this food running in and out of the kitchen, and these huge trays. It was like white noise, but I had never experienced that. It was really overwhelming. But it was really, really invigorating, too. I worked with him as a runner for about six months, then I became a server. Through this time, I realized that maybe going back home was not what I wanted to do, so I stayed for a year. And then at the year mark, I stayed for another year. And then after that second year I was like, "I'm not going back home." I knew it then. I had a strong enough voice, after being here for two years, to say, "I can take care of myself. I'm going to stay." So I did that.

But I never really thought that I was going to start a restaurant on my own. I knew I really liked people — I had a way of connecting with folks. I love food. I loved the moments and the experiences that we created at the restaurant. But I wasn't sure. At some point, I decided to go back to school and I got a major in fine arts and art history at UNC (University of North Carolina at Chapel Hill). I think that time in my life gave me an opportunity to see myself as an artist, and that I really wanted to be creating things. I did a lot of photography and inspirational work while I was in school. I met a lot of really interesting people. After I graduated, I couldn't really find anything to do that was inspiring to me. I got married through the process and I had my first kid.

Then Carlos said, "There is a chance to open up a lunch spot in downtown Raleigh. Do you want to look at it?" I think I was six months pregnant with my second child, but I said, "Okay." I knew once I became a mother I wanted to do something that I could leave as a legacy for my kids in terms of financial stability. Growing up that was not something that we had. I think that's what drove me to say to Carlos, "Yeah, let's go take a look at the spot and see what the possibilities are."

We put an offer on the building and it was denied. They took another offer. I had Ana, and then I think when Ana was six months they came back to us and said, "Are you guys still interested in the building?" We were in a position to do a better negotiation, and we ended up buying it. We decided that we were going to open this restaurant just for lunch. Little did I know what I had signed up for. As soon as word got out that we were going to open a location for Dos Taquitos in downtown Raleigh, people started saying, "Well, you can't just be open for lunch, you need to be open for dinner." So we started revisiting what that would look like.

Then Martha came into the picture. Martha was our chef for the first year the restaurant was open. She was from Panama and she was working with Carlos at the moment but there wasn't enough creative space for her. Bringing her into this new venture seemed like the most fitting situation for us. Then as we were under construction, Carlos reconnected with his high school sweetheart and decided that he could no longer live without this woman. So, he moved back to Colombia. I had all kinds of panic moments, because I had never opened a restaurant before. My youngest one had just turned a year old. I had a two-year-old – I was twenty-eight. He said, "Okay, I'm out. I know you can do it." And he left.

That was the biggest gift because even though I had no idea what I was doing, it gave me an opportunity. I've always been a believer that *necessity is the biggest space for creativity to happen*. I needed to make sure that it worked so I poured my heart and soul into this project.

Wow — that was a heck of a challenge in front of you! What did you do when he left?

I reached out to Ashley Christensen (owner of Ashley Christensen Restaurants). She was such an instrumental part of when we first opened, because she was opening Poole's at the same time. I think we opened in September and she opened Poole's in December. She had already had another restaurant then, and she had all this experience. She was just so generous with her time and her contacts and her life. I felt like, "I'm going to reach out to the people that I know, and we're just going to go to town and make this work." So we did the first year, and then Martha passed away.

She had battled with cancer since she was eighteen. This was an ongoing thing for her. She had periods of her life where she was very, very healthy, and then eight months into it she got really sick. We were trying to make it work so she could continue to help and be there. But, it was not what was going to happen. She passed and we were faced with the decision of what to do.

She had a sous chef but it was hard to work with him and he left soon after Martha passed. I remember sitting down with my cousin Nathalia, who worked with me until last year, and saying, "I have this idea that might work. If you would take over the front of the house, I will take over the kitchen. I think that we can make it work." I took over the kitchen the very next day and Nathalia took over the front of the house. I've **never worked so hard in my life** as those first three years.

Did you have experience running a kitchen?

I'd never run a kitchen in my life. I had a lot of creative input into what we were doing, just because I feel like the artist in me was really, really interested in all of what was happening. But not the day-to-day of running a kitchen. I remember talking to various people and asking for advice and just going with my gut.

We just took over and I started organizing things, putting structures in place and really understanding what it was that we were trying to do, how we were going to do it and why we were doing it. I think that's what drove me to work in the kitchen and to make it work for everybody else. We started having fun with it. It was a lot of hard work, but it was still a lot of fun. There was a lot of space for creativity for me there and to be the leader that I didn't know that I was going to be. I had no idea that this was going to be a possibility for me when I moved to the States. I found myself in a position where I could fully take charge and make a difference, even if it was just in the lives of the people that were involved in our project at the time.

So it worked in your favor to be on your own…

The restaurant would be a totally different place if he had been an active partner in the creation of what we do. Our day-to-day structures of how we run a shift, or how we keep inventory, or how we track schedules, I've been able to create that from what I think is best.

Did this create any challenges for you?

The biggest challenge of the restaurant at the beginning was that we named the restaurant Dos Taquitos Centro because we wanted to capitalize on the Dos Taquitos popularity. But our restaurant was nothing like Dos Taquitos. I think that there's a franchise understanding– like everything that is called the same should look the same, smell the same, be the same. If it's not, it appears deceiving and inconsistent.

Our menu is totally different. We've gone against something that all Mexican restaurants do in the United States which is giving free chips and salsa. I said, *"We're not doing that."* A lot of people when they think about eating Mexican food it's always this extra sense of fullness because you have overindulged in chips and salsa, and then you don't really enjoy your meal. Give yourself the opportunity to have space for dessert or enjoy another cocktail. It was a really, really intentional decision. There was a lot of backlash. But, we use higher quality ingredients in everything that we do, so for us it was not something that we could just write off. There were little things and big things that were decisions that I made that were different. It was just a different restaurant because he wasn't here. It was my opportunity to create this. As an artist that was great.

You had the courage to trust your instincts and the confidence to create something unique and not like everybody else's restaurant.

It's so much easier to see it now, eight years in the making. At the time I don't think I was able to recognize it as that — we were just doing. Just doing, doing, doing, doing, doing. It's been an interesting, full ride.

Talk about being a creative person in the restaurant business.

Somebody just called me the other day and said, "So, Angela, you're sort of like a visionary." I feel like as an artist, I am that. I have all these creative ideas. In my team I've always had integrators, and those are the people that actually get things done with the staff. That's been my biggest contribution, but also has been my biggest challenge. I have hundreds of ideas that I think we want to do but in reality putting things into practice, sometimes is not feasible.

I also have people in my team that hold me accountable and bring me back to the ground by saying, "Hey, these are amazing ideas but maybe we can't do these right now because of this and this and that. You need to prioritize." Being able to be the boss has been great, because I can speak what's on my mind and what's in my heart. And having a *team that holds me accountable* for what's actually possible in real life has been what's made us effective and efficient in what we're doing.

You bought your building. Was that important to you?

I don't think that it was important to me. What I knew coming into this partnership with Carlos was that I wanted to be able to be a partner. I had nothing to give him but my work. Whatever deal that we did I wanted to make sure that I was up to being a partner with him. I knew it was a possibility of investment and could help secure the future of the kids and the family. At the time it was easier for us to buy the property. Now I see the value of having made that decision.

A lot of big things that have happened in my life have happened out of chance, like moving to the States. A lot of relationships I have and a lot of people that I relate myself with happened by chance, by *believing that there are always possibilities*. I feel like the restaurant and the building are also on that same theme. It was sort of by chance, but I really, truly believed in it and threw myself into it. And now we have these properties in downtown Raleigh. If nothing else, it was a good investment for us.

And lease negotiations can be very challenging. Dos Taquitos had to move locations after twenty-three years in business because of a dispute with the landlord that could not be resolved. That has a huge impact on your business.

I understand you use as many local, fresh or organic ingredients as you can, right?

Yes, that's something else that we're really getting back to. The concept of the restaurant was how we could make this cuisine with local and organic ingredients in the area. We've danced around that for many years. "How do we make this work in terms of cost and profitability?" I have learned to do that in my journey as the main cook of this venture. In creating those relationships with people, we're learning how to make this sustainable. That's an ongoing evaluation. "How can we do things more effectively? Is this something that we can do all the time?" We realized that we can't. So we like to feature a lot of our special events with the relationships that we have with farmers in our local agriculture. I always continue to revise our menu so we can have those things in there. That's been one of my biggest learning curves as a person that manages the kitchen of this restaurant.

You got advice from others when you were starting out. Do others come to you now asking for advice and mentorship?

I feel like my first line of mentorship is my staff. I'm really intentional with everything that we do, so we really make a difference in the life of the people that work for us. Through the years it's been really beautiful to see that we are actually making a little bit of a difference in the people that work for us and the people that no longer work for us but worked for us at some point. They come back and share beautiful stories. I feel like I am more of a mentor to those folks than anything else.

I reach out to my community. I do a lot of work with the Boys & Girls Club, and in turn we now have people that used to be in their after-school program work for us. This is an ongoing conversation — creating spaces where there is the possibility to instill confidence in young folks.

I think a lot about that, because I have two young girls. I'm always trying to figure out what they need to learn so they can be amazing in whatever it is that they decide they want to do. Not successful, but just amazing so they can really, really be happy and thrive. I think after many, many, many conversations, that's been the conclusion. If we have a space where they can build confidence they can really take on anything.

What is it you hope that people who area a part of the Centro team take with them?

To not be afraid. To take what's there and run with it. To honor your talents. To learn how to work as a team and realize that there's really a lot of power in letting other people be part of your dream, or be part of this journey. How to be intentional every day when it comes to the shift, when it comes to your relationships, when it comes to everything. Just how to be intentional about who you are in the world, or who you are through your team, or who you are for your family. Because it makes a difference. Everything that you do and everything that you say to anybody in the world makes a difference. Sometimes that difference can really change their lives. It could be something little or it could be something huge. Make sure that the difference that you're making is a real difference, where you can move somebody into action so they can do whatever it is that they want to do like moving to another country or pursuing a different career or really taking on the possibility of recreating family and relationships. *Have an intentional life*. I feel like that's what's made the biggest difference in the way that we work.

Seth Gross

Bull City Burger and Brewery
DURHAM, NC

Pompieri Pizza
DURHAM, NC

RESTAURANT OWNER SINCE 2011

How'd you get into the restaurant business?

The quick story is I was cooking my way through high school. A chef took me under his wing and I said, "This is really great." I was supposed to go to college, and I remember coming home my senior and saying to my parents, "You know what? I want to be a chef." I was enamored by the life and the joking and the banter of the kitchen and the hard work. Their response was, "No way in hell are you going to spend the rest of your life working in kitchens, slaving away in the heat. You are going to college." So, to make them happy, I went to college and got a microbiology degree. When I graduated I had two applications – one to med school and one to the Culinary Institute of America. I didn't tell my parents about the CIA. I figured I'll send it in and if I get in, then I'll make a decision. I still had time to submit my medical application.

Well, two weeks literally to the day that I graduated from the University of Florida, I started at the CIA in Hyde Park, NY, and never really looked back. I never thought I'd use my microbiology degree, but I was cooking in Chicago and I used to hang out and drink beer at a little brew pub called Goose Island Brewery. I got to know Greg Hall, who was the head brewer and part owner along with his dad. He's a real foodie, and he would ask me about sauces and beer with food and wine with food. One day he said to me, "You know what? You have a great background that would be perfect for becoming a brewer. My assistant's leaving — do you want to learn to brew beer?" I was not very smart. I was still young and kind of dumb. But I was smart enough to know that everybody seemed to want this job, so I should take it and could always go back to cooking.

I'd never home-brewed or anything, but he took me in and taught me so much. It allowed me to go from there to becoming a sommelier. I travelled the world with wine, and then opened up a wine shop. Finally, I loved what I did but I always wanted to get back to that down-home beer idea, because I love making things by hand. And so, through wine I was able to meet investors who invested in me to open up Bull City Burger and Brewery. That was four-and-a-half years go. Now it's led to two restaurants and I'm planning on two more.

You have a clear mission statement and values. You really stand for something. What's behind that and why is it so important to you?

It's been a *slow evolution*. When I got out of cooking school I went to work for some top restaurants and chefs, and got exposed to a lot of interesting ingredients. At that time in the early 1990's, farmer's markets and CSAs [Community Supported Agriculture] were in their infancy. The exposure to these ingredients made me start to question some things. As I would meet some of these farmers and see ingredients roll in the back door I would say, "So, this is what this looks like." Someone would explain to me exactly why these tomatoes look different than what I'm used to seeing. Then I went to tastings and it all started to click, and I started to really question a lot about our food system.

Then you start reading, and that's always dangerous because you start learning — and then you realize, wait a second, what I'm doing is not good. I started learning about high fructose corn syrup and the possible detrimental effect to our health from that. And then trans fats. Then people like Michael Pollan start writing books and I started reading that stuff. And it all sort of came together. Then the pivotal moment for me, like with a lot of folks, was having kids. Then you start thinking about what is it that I'm doing that is going to make their future brighter, better. What am I going to leave behind?

I started thinking that we simply cannot enable the food system we have. Every week I have a food tour and I preach for about fifteen minutes, and I warn people that there's a low point. And when you think we're there, we're actually not – it gets worse. Then I bring people back up and say there's hope. And that hope is pasture-raised beef. We simply cannot continue on the path that we have. We feed America using so much corn, either through corn syrup and things like that in our diet, or through feeding livestock and all of the hormones and antibiotics that go with that. It is literally killing us slowly. I don't want to enable that. I wanted to *make a difference*.

The one thing that people do every day in our world is eat. If I want to effect change in my community, food is a great vehicle to make that voice. So we're not preachy, except for that Saturday sermon. We just sort of say, "Hey, we feature pasture-raised beef." If people are willing to ask, "Well, why?" then it gives me an opportunity to expand on that and give them some information. Most people come away saying "Wow, I had no idea! I wish someone had told me that."

I know it's hard. As a former user, you can't quit overnight. But you start at home. You start making changes in your diet. Then slowly, as you go out, you start to question where your food came from. If enough consumers out there are questioning these things and asking chefs to make changes in their menus and what they do, I think that there's a movement there and that's what I'm all about.

Tell me about the effects of "corn-fed" beef.

When we started changing cows from feeding on grass to corn, it had an enormous effect on everything in our lives, from our healthcare system to the way cars are built. All of it has been affected by corn. Changing the diet of the cow has had a huge impact on our health, because when a cow eats corn you have higher saturated fat, higher cholesterol, lower linoleic acid, lower omega fatty acids — and those two things fight cancer. In America we have more obesity, cancer, heart disease, strokes and diabetes than any nation on the planet, and a big part of that is definitely the meat that we've been eating. It's been a slow erosion of our health. We didn't see these effects prior to the 1970's when we moved to start feeding cows corn. I remind people that our beef is banned in the EU. It is against the law to feed a cow corn in Europe. You cannot take American beef to Europe — it is forbidden. In Europe they simply do not have the amount of health problems that we have, especially because of our meat and the amount of corn that is in people's diets.

I bet most people have no clue about this.

Absolutely. For forty years it's how we have been raised and what we have done. It's a paradigm shift for folks to think about.

But you stand for more than just pasture-raised beef...

Correct. At Bull City Burger and Brewery, we're the kind of restaurant that doesn't have tomatoes in January on our burgers because you can't grow tomatoes locally in January. I've been sent emails praising that and saying how amazing it is — "I can't believe you stand for that, this is so great." And I've had an equal number of people tell me they will never come back to the restaurant, they will never eat there again — "I hate this restaurant because you don't have tomatoes in January." I say, "Well, the tomatoes are mealy, they're hard, and they don't taste good." I've literally had customers say to me, "I don't care. A tomato belongs on a burger."

At the heart of that is how we have become as a society and a culture. We have become enabled to think food should be available all the time, year-round, no matter what we want. There isn't a blame necessarily on people for that. We have huge food companies that have completely changed the American diet and have absolutely manipulated what we eat and how we do, because it was easy for them. So, it's funny how a lot of people kind of accepted that corn isn't always available. It's really a seasonal food — it's a summer thing. We look to sweet corn when it's delicious eating corn in the summer. We don't necessarily expect it unless it comes out of a can in January. But with tomatoes, in America you should have something red in your salad twelve months of the year. Otherwise there is something wrong with your restaurant. It's just not how nature works.

We definitely need to educate people. When you pose the question to people and you say, "Look, Thanksgiving comes once a year. Christmas comes once a year. It's just how it is." You kind of joke and sort of lead them into this understanding that with your food, there's *advantages to eating seasonally*. You get to look forward to things that are really exciting and delicious when they're in season. Then you don't get bored of things. When strawberries are in season, I gorge on them for about six-to-eight weeks when they're really delicious and good. After that, strawberry season is over. And there's something else that's coming around the corner. You get all excited on that. But, strawberries are not something we should be eating year-round. You look at how does that get to the table in January, and it doesn't taste good anyway. There's a real kind of "aha" moment for some people when they go, "You know, I never thought about that."

What toppings do you use during the winter months?

It gets hard. At Pompieri Pizza we joke that if you like brussel sprouts, you're going to love it here in the winter because we do a lot of brussel sprout pizzas and these kale pizzas and things that do well in this colder weather. That's just how it is. If you come in in February and you think you're going to see zucchini and tomatoes on a pizza, it just isn't going to happen. We just aren't going to do that. We're trying to work with local farmers. I like that food should be traceable, that you know it's accountable.

We use different things to make that point. At Bull City, it's the tomatoes. Granted, we still have caramelized onions on the menu but we simply cannot just get rid of everything that isn't seasonal, such as garlic and onions. We just use tomatoes as a way to communicate that message. But, for the most part, on a burger, most of the things that we have are grown locally. Lettuce can be grown in the winter in the greenhouse. I'm kind of finicky that way, too. Yes, you can find tomatoes that are local in January, except they're grown in a greenhouse using fossil fuels and they don't taste good. I just won't support that. But lettuce is something that can grow without fossil fuels in greenhouses.

So, it's a fine line. It strikes a debate. **What is local?** You want to open up a can of worms, you start talking about what is local. I live in Durham. Our restaurants are in Durham. If I buy lettuce in Durham we would all pretty much agree that's local. If I go a few miles toward Raleigh and we buy lettuce there, is that local? A lot of people would say, "Yeah, that's still pretty local. Some people would say, "Well, that's not so local." If we go several hours away to Wilmington, is that local? Well, now it's not so local. Where do you draw that line? If I want coffee beans, there's no North Carolina coffee beans. We've got to go to South America for coffee.

How do you make those determinations?

Drawing these lines is a crucial thing. At the end of the day I have to go to sleep at night and think about what am I comfortable with and where can I draw those lines. There are some things I simply won't compromise on. For instance, I will close the restaurant before I'll serve corn-fed beef. There's no gray area for me there. I know the farmers that I get our beef from. I've walked these farms. I've seen them. I've seen the cows. I've dined with these farmers at their table and at our restaurant. The relationship is solid and we're all committed to the same movement and that's really important.

I admire your approach. It's clear you stand for something.

You can't be everything to everybody. There are restaurants that try to do that. If you try to do that, good luck. That's a tough road to go. You end up having to **cut corners and compromise**, because simply trying to please everybody is just a losing proposition to me. Those are the menus, typically at a diner or something, where it's a seventeen-page plastic thing that you flip through, and they serve breakfast all day long, lunch all day, dinner all day. You've got to wonder just how fresh it is if they're serving omelets and meatloaf and spaghetti and pancakes and all of these things.

But if you like burgers, we make twenty-eight different toppings in-house. The hot sauce, the Worcestershire sauce, sriracha, mayonnaise, mustard, barbecue sauce – everything but the ketchup is literally made in the restaurant. With that, you've got a lot of options. We have a number on the website and it's kind of just a weird number that sits out on some of the pages. It says 67,108,864. That's the number of hamburgers you can make with twenty-eight different toppings. So, if you like burgers, you're in the right place.

At Pompieri Pizza, we do wood-fired Neapolitan style pizzas. That's about it. We have a few appetizers. We make gelato. But it really wasn't about "Hey, let's add pasta to it" and "Let's do panini sandwiches and ravioli and all these things." I want to make really good burgers and I want to make really good pizza. And that's what we stand for. I'd rather do *quality over quantity*. That has always been the mission. If you're not in the mood for pizza, that's okay. Hopefully you are next week or the week after and you'll come in. I just don't want to have the steak and fish entrée and all these different things, because as soon as you dilute the menu, I feel like quality begins to drop.

Is it hard to find staff who believe in your mission?

First of all, the staff is absolutely one of the best things about these restaurants. They are fantastic folks who work really hard. They do believe in the mission. Those who come onboard know we do something with our food, but they're not real sure. And after a short period of going through some training and sitting with me and learning, it's a pretty remarkable transformation. We have an employee who talks about how she had gone to a family picnic after working with us for a year. At the family picnic during summer they were making burgers. She took one bite of the burger and couldn't eat it. Now this is a girl who probably shops at Food Lion and had never ever in her life considered where her food came from. But just being an employee and eating our food on a regular basis, she started to make that transformation for herself and her children. I think that's a really powerful thing.

The employees are just fantastic in what they bring to the table, how they become so passionate about the mission and sharing it, and how they're willing to educate customers from what they're learning.

Tell me about the "Tattoo Promise."

We have six people who have gotten tattoos with our logo or the name "Bull City Burger and Brewery." It was just sort of something that I had seen done a long time ago, and I filed it away as something I'd love to do someday to see if there was that much brand loyalty. So we decided that we would offer this tattoo promise, and if anybody actually did it they would get a discount for life. I'm shocked that there are six people and I'm thrilled at the same time. We can never close the restaurant now because these people have tattoos. So I plan to be here a long time, and they're pretty loyal customers. But it was all done in good fun. It certainly gets a lot of talk. Folks come in and see this — we've got it posted around the restaurant. You hear the jokes and all that. But these folks, they're really proud. They come in and they love to lift their shirt and show their stomach or wherever they've gotten it and show off that they have a Bull City tattoo. Then they get their discount. It's just been a real fun thing to see.

Let's go back to when you started. Did you already know your investors?

They were my wine shop investors. They said, "If you ever want to do anything else, we would love to back you."

I was lucky in that respect. I didn't have to spend a lot of time going out trying to find money and investors. I know that can be a really tough road. I did that for the wine shop, where I had to find a group of people who were willing to invest in that. But, once you prove yourself once, it gets a lot easier the second time around. That's always a trick. How do you find somebody who believes in your dream as much you?

There are several types of investors. There are people investing in something purely for the return. I've done well enough that I think that my investors are happy with the return. But I think because we are all passionate about the food we make and cook when we're in the restaurant industry, I would recommend finding people who are *passionate about the mission of your restaurant* and what your goals are, rather than just purely investment. First of all, if it doesn't go as well as you'd hoped, hopefully they say, "Well, the return is not good enough but we really love what you're doing and that's okay." And second, if they are as passionate as you and get the mission and they're invested in that, it makes conversation a bit easier, and they're out there as spokespeople and marketing and advertising for you as well. It just makes a better environment because they come in and they get as excited as you are to see that fresh foraged morels just came in the back door, or the fish that just came in from the coast that was literally caught at two a.m., and here it is ten a.m., it's in the restaurant and we're starting to butcher it. If someone gets excited about that they're probably a great investor to have on board.

So, that would be my choice. Always try to find someone who not only wants to see a good investment financially, but really gets what you're after and is excited as you are about the food.

What's your plan for the future?

I'm looking at least two more restaurants and there's a potential for five down the road if the plan goes well. But, each is a unique individual concept with a different food theme. We will always work with local farmers on sustainability and we're always focused on doing something well rather than lots of different things.

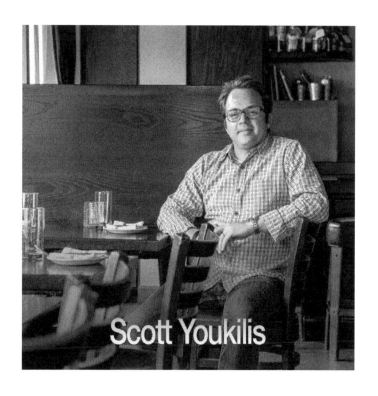
Scott Youkilis

Hog & Rocks
SAN FRANCISCO, CA

Loma Brewing Company
LOS GATOS, CA

RESTAURANT OWNER SINCE 2005

Tell me about your background and what prompted you to get involved in the restaurant business.

I was born and raised in Cincinnati. I went to school at Indiana and got a bachelor's degree. In high school and college, I was just working restaurants. My uncle owns a couple of restaurants and had been in the restaurant business for a bunch of years in Manhattan, so I got to see what he was doing and just somehow I got drawn to it. I also worked at one of the most popular, biggest family-owned restaurants in Cincinnati – Montgomery Inn. It was just a cool experience and I got drawn in. I still to this day don't know exactly how that happened, but it just did.

I had been cooking at home and for friends, but working more front-of-the-house. I decided that maybe culinary school would be a good option for me to round out my knowledge and experience. So, I went to Johnson & Wales in Providence, RI. It was a pretty easy decision between CIA (Culinary Institute of America) and Johnson & Wales, who were the two leaders in the late 90's. Johnson & Wales seemed more appealing because it was more business-focused. The culinary arts part was important and the creativity and the skills and all that were good, but they somehow looped in the business aspect really nicely. I worked weekends in New York when I could at my uncle's restaurant, and I finished school in a year-and-a-half. I decided I could stay in New York and the East Coast or move to San Francisco where I had a bunch of friends and be at the epicenter. I decided maybe San Francisco would be a better move – closer to wine country, closer to where all the food comes from. I ended up making that move in 2000 and line-cooked for a year. I moved to Tahoe, worked up there for year, and came back.

I made a good friend who ended up becoming my future business partner. We opened Maverick, my first restaurant, in 2005 — a thirty-five to forty seat restaurant. I was a chef and my partner was the general manager and sommelier. It was seven days a week, fifteen hour days for five years or something. The restaurant was a huge learning experience in life and restaurants and business, and we came out of the gates pretty strong. In 2006 we were named Best New Restaurant by *San Francisco Magazine* readers' poll. The same year we won Best Brunch, and we won that for about five to six more years. We were doing a great job, and we did it all the way until the end, until 2013, when we had our kitchen fire and that pretty much ended that. It was a good eight-year run. In 2010, we opened Hog & Rocks. I ended up finding a different partner. The guys approached me and thought we'd do a good job working together, so we opened it together. July 1 (2016) was our six-year anniversary.

How would you weigh learning from the classroom and culinary school versus having to roll up your sleeves and learn from trial and error?

I think the business is all about rolling up your sleeves. That's where the real learning is — the culinary part of it, especially. You're cooking every day. That's where you're going to learn. That's where you're making mistakes, you're having successes, you're putting plates together, and getting instant feedback from guests. That's when you know if things are working or not. Whether you're an owner or you're just a line cook and your chef is telling you you're doing a great job or you're doing a terrible job – that's where I think the learning is.

Culinary school was great. I know it's changed a lot over the years, but there was a good amount of discipline that was instilled in us. You have to be disciplined to be a good cook and to eventually be a good chef. You run a kitchen — there are a lot of rules you have to set for yourself and expectations that are made for you. There were a set of rules the school impressed upon you, but you're really not going to know and understand that until you're in the kitchen every night, or on the floor, behind the bar every night, and having that repetition and practice. It's a constant evolving thing. I'm over twenty years in the business now and it's still something new every day.

Culinary school has exploded in popularity and it's become a very expensive investment. What are your thoughts on taking that route for people starting out today?

I've asked people who are trying to think about it, "Have you worked in a restaurant before?" Because I came across people that had never worked in a restaurant before and I said, "Well, maybe you should work in a restaurant, or work for a catering company. Do it first and see what it feels like. Any restaurant these days will take you." If you can do that and you say, "This is for me, I'm into it," then I would consider the financial burden. Then ask good questions. Call people and find out, "Hey, what are people paying in that town that you live in?" In certain places like San Francisco, if you take on that kind of debt and the cost of living is so incredibly high and the wages aren't that much better than if you're living in Denver or Saint Louis or Charlotte, how do you pay that debt back?

I'm not sure where the culinary schools stand now in terms of job placement, but it was always that false sense of becoming a sous chef, or having this high paying salary right out of school. *That's just not the case*. I don't know if they've pulled back from that, but you've got to work for that.

Your first job was a line cook?

I was foolish to think I could actually be a sous chef and then I figured out that's not going to work. No one would hire me. And I was fine with that. My goal was actually just to be a chef-owner. I didn't want to work for a big corporation or a huge hotel chain. I wanted to work for a person who I could see myself being in five or ten years. Even if I got paid a little bit less, I knew that I wanted to be part of that small team and neighborhood restaurant because I knew that's what I wanted to be someday.

I'd always been attracted to small business. My dad ran his own business for nearly twenty years and there was something that seemed very tangible and something that I could actually acquire at some point in time – not realizing at seventeen years old how much actual money, how much effort and time it took to get to that point. But there's something about seeing the owners there almost every night, even if it was just for an hour or just stopping in, checking in and saying "Hi" to people and the staff, making sure everyone was good. It felt very genuine. It was something I could kind of hold onto and it seemed to be real.

Tell me about starting Maverick.

We scraped every penny we could get together, two hundred and fifty thousand, all in, and we purchased the business. It was thriving in that space and they had done so well that they moved down the street and opened a bigger space but kept that one open as a restaurant called LeMone. It became a very successful Peruvian restaurant in San Francisco and they've been doing it for a bunch of years. We knew we were moving to a good location in terms of a successful business there, but it was not the cleanest, nicest part town. We had some complications early on with the locals. The end of Mission Street could be pretty rough. We got it for a good deal, but we had a loan through the mayor's office for the business loan. We had some private loans from friends and family, and we had investors come in. We threw up some of our own money. We did a lot of the work ourselves and opened up and remodeled in a little less than three months.

We were off to the races. We were busy from day one. We only had a beer and wine license, so it was much cheaper. Now with Hog & Rocks, we had to buy a liquor license. We bought a liquor license for seventy thousand dollars in 2009, and now they're up to two hundred and fifty thousand dollars just for a liquor license. I paid two hundred and fifty thousand to open a forty-seat restaurant, all in, and now it costs the same amount of money just to get the license. It's an asset, it's your greatest asset, but it's a really big cost.

It would seem like that just eliminates the opportunity of even thinking about a restaurant in San Francisco for many people.

I know. It's a lot. But the competitive market dictates that. You've got one of the most if not *the* most competitive markets for restaurants maybe anywhere — certainly in the U.S. and probably in much of the world. There is a lot of money out here. There's no shortage of that. Restaurants continue to open every day. It doesn't seem to slow down. If you read the news, *Eater* or the *San Francisco Chronicle* in the Food & Wine sections, big name guys are closing and opening and closing and opening. Everyone always talks about how many restaurant openings there were this year, or last year. But everyone forgets how many actually close. We're seeing growth but it continues to level itself out. The scary part is raising a million, a million-and-a-half dollars and seeing your restaurant close the doors nine months later. That's scary stuff. That's a lot of risk and that's a lot of money to lose quickly.

If you were raising money today, where would you go? How would you structure a deal that would be attractive to investors?

We're doing that with Loma now. My brother's kind of a big name so he attracted some guys, and it is kind of about who you know. But I think you have to have a little balance. You've got to bring on some debt, you've got to bring on some equity.

What's a good split?

I don't know. I think it just depends. I know guys that just do all debt. That could be a big line item in your expenses every month. But if you can make it work, you make it work. You're profitable and those distributions are going straight into your pocket. But you can't do that on number one. I can only imagine if you're putting up your whole entire house and all your savings and every bit of collateral that you have to get a million bucks from a bank. In a market like San Francisco, how do you even get to that? How do you line cook and afford a house?

I know a lot of other markets where you can be a line cook or a server and own a house. You're not likely to do that in San Francisco. It's hard to make that jump. You have to pull all your resources together, have a good couple of partners, and have a good network. It would be nearly impossible to do it on your own here. There's no way you would know enough people and have the time to do that. The advantage of having my partner Mike, who did Maverick, was that we had our own pools of people. You just spread that network as far as you can and hopefully you can get it all together. It was so much different ten years ago than it is now, mostly because the numbers are so much bigger.

What have you learned from having business partners?

Having partners in business — I don't care what industry you're in — it's probably one of the *hardest parts of owning a business*. The best side of having a partner is that you have someone to collaborate with. Sometimes it's nice to bounce ideas off each other. Good partnerships work where you're bringing in different things to the table and then there are some compromises and agreements and you can really move forward faster. If everything's pointed at yourself, you're it.

With a restaurant, it's constant every day that you're having to make decisions. It can be quite tiresome. You can balance that with someone like I did with Kevin — I'll run the back of the house and you run the front of the house. If we split up and divide and conquer, we'll be in better shape. The hard part is that when you start to butt heads or you start to count hours. God forbid you'd end up coming to that. But those are real issues that people come up with where you're like, "I'm here fifteen hours a day and you're only here five hours a day, and we're getting paid the same. What the hell is that all about?" We didn't really run into those issues so much. But for those looking to get into it, get someone on your side you can trust to be there. If you have to step out or you have a family and you want to go on a trip, you know that things are going to run as well as if you're there. You're gone and you can rely on each other. My partners now are less on the restaurant side of things. They've left it up to me to be the operations guy, which is great. I've had to lean on my managers and chefs to be there for me and rely on them, which is great, too, because they're all amazing and they've all been dedicated and very talented. They're all looking to continue on and learn as they go. But partnerships? I think it's one of the hardest parts of the business.

Do you recommend having previously worked with somebody if you're going to get in a partnership with him or her?

It can be advantageous for sure to have worked with someone before. If you are side-by-side with that person in the weeds, busy Friday night — nothing's going right — you you see how people react to that. I think that's usually a good indicator of what it's going to be like if we own that business together. But, it's only an indicator of what happens in that moment because there are other stresses and other problems are going to come in when you own the business.

I'm in there with my brother now at Loma. He's new to the restaurant business, and he's been great because he's open. He's listening and he's trying to absorb as much as he can, as fast as he can. He's going to go through a whole change in perspective in how our restaurants are and how they're going to be — the highs and the lows and how do you deal with them. It'll be interesting to see how he adapts to it. For me and for my general manager and my chefs who have been in the business for a long time and have been part of opening teams, we know what to expect. He doesn't. Generally speaking, I think it's probably a good idea to get to know that person pretty well and see what they're like in the heat of things.

Have you been able to find a sustainable balance between work and life outside of work?

I've had some good people working for me. Operationally, I've set it up now so people know what the expectations are from the interview. When you come in and you want to interview for the assistant manager or the general manager or the chef's job, I say, "This is what's expected of you because this is who I am and this is what this place is all about." That's helped pull me away and mostly it's allowed me to expand the current brand. It allows me to do those things and it becomes attractive to an incoming chef or an incoming manager or a server or a bartender. *There's growth here*. There's more to this. If I'm in the weeds every night cooking, if I'm behind the stove every day, where are we going to go? How are we going to move forward? And, in a place like San Francisco, it's hard to survive on one restaurant, so you have to think about how you're going to continue to grow. And restaurants, they're quick. Forget how many restaurants die in a year or never make it past one year. How many restaurants make it past ten years? I think they're not meant to last that long. They're trendy, they're a moment in time. A lot of times restaurants will be open ten years and they'll just close up shop and they might have ten years left on their lease. Maybe they were Italian and now say, "Let's do

Mexican. Let's do something new. Let's reinvigorate it. We still owe rent but our profits have slowed down. Let's try something brand new. And maybe we can do better." I think there's a short lifespan for many reasons. I think a lot of them are good reasons. I don't think there's anything wrong with changing things up and keeping it fresh and new. Who wants to keep something tired and old?

Instead of just investing into making ongoing tweaks or changes, it can be beneficial to close up and start fresh?

It could be. It takes a lot of capital to do that. If that's a problem, it could be an issue. If you don't have the money, you can't do that. But maybe it doesn't take that much money. You've got a kitchen. You've got a bar. Maybe a facelift and a new name and usually it works. I don't know if that works in every market. I know in big cities it can happen because there's just so much change so quickly and the density of people. I've known that to work for people. They literally change their name and change their menu and paint the walls different and reopen. It's worked. It doesn't work for everyone, mostly because I think not everyone is talented enough and creative enough to do that. It takes a lot of guts. *Change is scary.*

Hog & Rocks has been open for six years. What have you done to try to keep it fresh and keep existing customers coming in while attracting new folks?

It's a challenge. I've had a great PR and marketing team for years and that's what we talk about almost all the time. How do we continue to keep ourselves fresh and new and in the media? Even if it's just a little hit here and there, how do you do that? We've been successful. *San Francisco Magazine* just came out and we were named "Best Cocktail Bar in San Francisco." I hired a new bar manager in December and he came on board and revamped the menu, added a bunch of new drinks, kept the core of our whiskey program and what was intact and what was working. I said, "Look, there are some things here that are not broken. We're doing great things here but I want you to put your touches on it." And so he did. He brought a great new energy. He has amazing energy and we brought new people on that are continuing to feed off of his energy and bring a much stronger bar program. And, hey, what do you know? *San Francisco Magazine*'s hot for us, so great! A new chef came in last year. My chef had been on for three years and he left to go on to other great things, and so a new guy comes on. What do you know? He came in, kept the core as I directed. But I said, "There are great things that are not broken and things that could be changed. I want you to put your own touches on it and own it." He's a

"Rising Star Chef" in *San Francisco Chronicle*. People are excited. He's doing new things. There's something about keeping the blood flowing.

The concept I put together from the beginning is timeless. We've been eating oysters for hundreds of years. Cured meats, ham, prosciutto, serrano — these things have been made and eaten for hundreds of years. They're not going out of style. A good burger, a good gastro-pub fare — those are the things people just want all the time. So we won't have to do much. Maybe interiors have to change to spruce things up. You've got to do a new paint job. New artwork, eventually. Redo things if you feel like that's the case. But think about things in a timeless manner, things that won't go out of fashion, and I think you can be successful. But don't be boring. You don't want to do the same old thing that everyone else is doing. I don't know where we will be in four years or ten years. Maybe I'll just get bored and say we don't want to eat oysters anymore.

Tell me about finding great people to work for you — that seems to be an issue for every owner I speak to.

It's hard. It's really hard. I mentioned earlier the cost of living in San Francisco is tough. Our minimum wage is going up. It's harder to do business in the city than it's ever been, but it's also more attractive for the best talent in the world. Who wouldn't want to work at a great restaurant in San Francisco? We have the advantage that a lot of really talented people want to come through San Francisco. They want to work here. They want to make good money. They want to experience it. And then, maybe they take it home or they go to the next town. It's a pretty transient group of people that work in restaurants. Finding them and holding onto them is hard. It will always be an issue.

I don't know what the graduation rate for people coming out of culinary school these days is, but I think there's less and less people doing that than there used to be. I think a lot of people just want to skip a step. They don't want to get down and dirty and start from the bottom and work their way up anymore. It might be a ***generational issue***. As a chef you have to be creative in terms of how you set up a restaurant. So, if you don't have as many talented people around and your labor pool is lower, maybe you won't have a six-man cooking line. Maybe you need to come up with a restaurant that has a three-man line. Or if you can only find two bartenders that can measure and care about making a good cocktail, maybe you should have a smaller bar and only have two wells.

What are you looking for when you hire?

Mostly the personality, especially the front of the house. We have a fun place and people come in a lot, a couple times a week. It's a neighborhood place. You've got to be smiling, you've got to be cordial. You need to care about people. You can usually tell a lot of that early in the interview, the kind of person they are. That's usually the good starting point. Someone I can actually have a good conversation with about anything, and get along with, and who is passionate about the industry. Quality people, that's usually where I start. There's a lot of things to be learned, but you *can't learn hard work and personality*. Those things are your core. I get those things first and then look at experience.

At the same time, we've had issues with servers recently where they're maybe just a little too green or they're not ready to work in a restaurant that has a pretty complex menu and there's two hundred and fifty bottles of booze on that back wall. There's a lot of stuff to know. If you've never worked in a place that is demanding of you on that level, then we can only coach you so much. I'm willing to give people a chance, but, you have to want it. You can't just walk in a place like ours and say, "Yeah, I'm going to work here Friday nights. I'm going to be a server now." You're not ready for that — not even close. It's harder than it used to be but I think that ten years ago it was still hard to find people that you can really trust.

Do you let people who don't cut it go quickly?

Unfortunately, I'm probably too quick to release. I lose patience. We've also been too quick to hire, too. Probably another fault. You need someone quick and you're like, "Well, let's take a chance." It seems to never work out. Restaurants require a lot of manpower, so sometimes you just need bodies. It's a constant thing. We've been talking about that a lot more. We need more training time early on and more coaching in the moment. But, it's hard sometimes.

On the financial side of the business, do you spend a lot of time focused on ways to save money?

We watch the numbers a lot. I do all the bookkeeping. I look at every invoice. Technology has increased tremendously and it's helped us a lot. It's just really been making things easier to track. *Waste is the number one way to lose money*, of course. We keep pretty tight track of it. We have our struggles sometimes and our cost of goods include a pretty luxurious list of ingredients for our menus. Trying to pass it off in value at neighborhood-friendly prices is hard. But, we're in San Francisco, so we have to make money. We're not handing it out.

How do you deal with negative reviews? Or do you just focus on the business and let that stuff take care of itself?

We do read them all. And I think it's important to read them all. I think some people are unnecessarily mean. I don't know why. Maybe they just had a bad day. Okay. Sorry I made it worse or didn't make it better. Then we weren't doing our job. But I think ultimately it's really hard to worry about what people think about you. I can't change that. There's only so much I can do to do that. What we can do and what I tell the staff all the time is that, "Hey, that drink might have taken twenty minutes, or maybe you came across a little unfriendly to that person and they took it the wrong way. Whatever the case is, maybe we did do that. But, what we need to focus on is the things that we can do. Is the food seasoned right? Is it hot? Are the drinks cold. Did they come out quickly? Were we friendly?" Those are things we have complete control of and those are things I can actually manage. If we manage those things well, then the end result will come out in positive Yelp reviews and positive critiques of the restaurants from professionals or media. Those things I can control. I can't control how someone got fired, or broke up with their girlfriend and they came in bitter and decided, "You know what? I'm going to take it out on these guys." I get it. It's cool. It's the world we live in now. I don't let it hurt me. It's fine. We're still doing alright. We're still busy. We're still open.

It sounds like you've made a good investment in PR which you can use in a positive way. Is it more important in a market like San Francisco? Or do you think it's just a good investment in general?

It's probably almost a necessary thing in San Francisco to compete on a high level. I don't know what it would be like to not have it. I always dream about not spending that money — we would save so much money. But then there's that fear of if we pulled this thing at this point, six years later, *what happens*? Who's going to manage it? There's still a lot on social media and newsletters and media requests, and when we want to announce a new thing someone has to do that.

They're a very valuable resource, and they're great. They're friends and colleagues and they're great people. I would say in a smaller market it might not be as necessary. But, the stakes are getting higher. It's cheaper to open a restaurant in Charlotte, I'm sure, than it is in San Francisco. But there's still a competition and there's still money involved. It's still a business and you don't want to fail. So, you've got to figure what you can afford and try not to overspend and try to be smart about how you spend that money. But the PR thing and marketing has been huge. I'd rather spend the money on people doing the work and being in contact with people than just throwing a billboard up or throwing an ad in the newspaper. I've actually done a little bit of Facebook ads that have been pretty good — very cheap, but they reach a lot of people. I don't know if anyone walks in from using traditional print media. Do they bring a coupon in? How do you know? There are so many people that are on their phones, on social media, reading the blogs, reading all the food stuff so we continue to keep the PR team focused on that and we'll keep our name out there. That's money well-spent.

Is there anything you want to share with people getting started in the business?

It's a tough business. For someone who is thinking about making that step, just make sure you do a lot of research and a lot of homework and figure out whether or not you're ready. Make sure you have enough money, because I don't care what city you're in or what business you're in, *if you're undercapitalized, you're done for*. It's being prepared and understanding the risks that are involved. It can be a very, very great experience. It can be a very, very bad situation, too. So be careful.

Bida Manda

Brewery Bhavana

TWO LOCATIONS ACROSS TWO CONCEPTS -
RALEIGH, NC

RESTAURANT OWNER SINCE 2012

Tell me about your background.

We opened the restaurant on September 1, 2012. It was just my sister, Vanvisa, and I. We never really intended to open a restaurant. I went to NC State and did design and chemistry. I had a graduate degree in international peace and conflict studies from Trinity in Dublin, Ireland. I never thought that we would be in the food industry. But it's amazing the journey your life takes.

So, after Trinity I came back to Raleigh and I was really just looking for jobs in international peace and conflict studies, in community building in general. And it was right around recession time, so I applied to about three hundred jobs in what was probably the hardest, the most difficult year of my life. *I got zero job offers.* None. So Vanvisa and I took a summer off that year and went to Laos and spent that summer with Mom and Dad. We just really reconnected with our roots.

When Vanvisa and I initially came to the U.S., I was twelve and she was nine. The rest of our family was still living in Laos. We left home at such a young age, so it was easy to assume that Laos was a long distant past. But what we realized now that we were older was that we are a direct part of that Laotian community. And looking back, food has always been so centered to my life. When Vanvisa and I arrived, we lived with an American family and the only way to make sure that her memories of home, of Laos, of mom and dad, were preserved as a small nine-year-old child was for me to cook for her. We couldn't just go to a Laotian restaurant. We couldn't just go to a Laotian temple. There's no Laotian community center anywhere. So, knowing all of that I knew I had to do something to make sure that she remembered home, and food was the most direct and most meaningful tool I had. Growing up with Mom and Dad, I always cooked. I think as a culture in general, cooking is almost a sacred, spiritual experience. It was such a privilege and honor to be able to share that experience with my sister.

Looking back now, it kind of makes sense that we are in this industry. But at the time of career choices, that was not the most obvious one.

Did I hear you correctly … you applied to 300 jobs and got no offers?

Yes. Even with all of those degrees and experiences, I got zero offers. It was everything from applying to the U.N., to applying to small MGOs working on educational empowerment in Guatemala. I got so desperate, I remember applying to work at CVS to be an assistant clerk. I think my resume can be perceived as a very distracted person. But, it has definitely led into a wonderful journey.

Considering you now have one of the best restaurants in Raleigh, it's quite an amazing journey!

I try to be sensitive to what it means to have a "best restaurant." I think we are definitely learning a lot. And I think the most fascinating thing for us is that what we do at Bida Manda really is just an extension of who we are. Our menu is nothing more than the dishes we remember eating growing up, the kind of dishes that I cooked for my sister to make sure that she remembers home. It's not a creative process. It's just a *genuine offering from our family to our community* here. It has been a very empowering journey to see that what we do is meaningful to the community and the community celebrates our narrative and authenticity to our food.

Let's start from the beginning. How did you begin the process of opening your restaurant?

The first stop when we came back to Raleigh was I went to Barnes & Noble and I bought a phenomenal book that's called *Opening a Restaurant for Dummies* (laughs). It really was that fundamental. We did not know **anything**. We did not know how we were going to look for space. We didn't know how we were going to look for funding. How are we going to find a chef? What is the legal complexity of it? So, we really started from scratch. I remember coming back and just kind of being shocked about the kind of resources in the community that were lacking at the time. How *do* you open a restaurant?

We were fortunate at that time to have the kind of relationships in Raleigh that allowed that to be a positive journey. I remember emailing Ashley Christensen and saying, "I would love to learn from you. Can you please mentor us?" I remember reaching out to Chris Powers at Trophy Brewing. I remember emailing Angela Salamanca, the owner of Centro. She's from Colombia and one of my closest friends now. I said, "This is my hope and dream and passion and heartbeat. I would love to learn as much as I could from you." And surprisingly, all of these successful, meaningful leaders in the food community said, "Yes!" And it all started with saying, "I love what you do and would love for you to be a part of this journey. Please train us. Teach us all you know."

Those are very well-respected, successful restaurant people in Raleigh. It says a lot that they offered to help.

The response was "We are so excited that you're passionate about Laotian food and your family narrative and your love of people. Let's make sure this happens." And I think that positive seed, that supportive tone, really changed how we approached the process. Instead of it being a business journey, it really was about *relationship building*.

From not knowing anything about the industry, we were granted so many relationships with people who know. I think the humility of saying "I don't know" and "I would love to know more" really opened a lot of opportunities and positive relationships in our lives. And that is something that we will forever treasure. That's how it all how it all began.

I was also fortunate to have a very supportive and loving group of friends. A lot of things from the construction of the space to a lot of the legal help to graphic design were donated and volunteered by our friends. We always use the visual image of our sticks on the wall that were completely hand-tied by our friends. We had about fifty of our friends working on that. We didn't have much funding so I gave all of them a Miller Light and we really just built the space together.

I think our guests can see a lot of the passionate hands that were involved in the making of the space, that are still important and meaningful to us today. Bida Manda is nothing but a reflection of what a tremendous, positive, loving community we have in Raleigh.

The hospitality at Bida Manda is phenomenal. What are you doing to provide that kind of atmosphere consistently?

I think the consistency is difficult and especially providing an intimate, meaningful, personal experience each and every time. That's very difficult in any restaurant. At Bida Manda we serve more than three thousand meals a week — how do we create that kind of consistency? It's an ongoing challenge. But our goal wasn't to be wealthy — our goal wasn't to create the best restaurant in Raleigh. Our goal was to make sure that we share our narrative, food and culture with our community the best that we know how.

I think it's that authenticity to what you love and allowing that to be the beginning of every decision-making process. Then it will always be something that's *organic and true*. I think "hospitality" is an interesting word because for us it really is us hosting and welcoming people into our home. It doesn't get any simpler than that. Food is such a basic life offering. When we overcomplicate that experience, that's when it gets tricky. For us it really is about how we continue sharing our story and welcoming our guests to our home, and caring for them like we were caring for our friends. That is our basic principle at the restaurant. We try to care for our friends and family and community.

It's your story and your narrative and it's very personal to you and Vanvisa. How do you share it through your staff?

I think sourcing the right team is probably the most important ingredient in what we do. How do we create a team that's cohesive and creative and fires all together to yield this experience? We spend a lot of time on the front-end of the selection process. We put a lot of attention and resources into that beginning phase of training and recruiting. It is so important to us that it doesn't matter if that person does not even have service industry experience. What we are looking for is always someone who's capable of caring — someone who is genuinely passionate about life. And that doesn't have to be food. We have a lot of artists. We have a lot of "makers" in the world. We have a Yoga instructor. We have a lot of students who are waiting to go to medical school. We have last year law school students. We are looking for people who are passionate in what they do, and in turn, they bring that aliveness to what we do and it adds a level of complexity and meaning to what they do.

"Intention" is the big word in our training process. And intention is actually really hard to train someone that doesn't already carry that sense of pride in what they do. How do we make polishing glasses as meaningful of an experience as talking to a guest at a table? What we have learned is that when we find someone that takes a lot of pride and meaning in what they do and love what they do, that translates directly to our guests' experience. We have such a phenomenal team and community at the restaurant that I'm so grateful for.

I think a lot of our success comes directly from that team. Developing and co-creating that team is very important to us. A good example is we take our *annual staff retreat once or twice a year*. We take three or four days off from the restaurant, and we spend some time somewhere else. The first year we went to Asheville in the N.C. mountains, and last year we went to Wilmington on the N.C. coast. It's just really allowing our team to go through a shared experience, setting intentions and goals, and showing them how to work for each other's development. We are just a community of passionate people who are just absolutely in love with what we do, and wanting to care for our guests.

Do you close the restaurant for a few days when you do this?

Yes, we do. It's always a few of the best days of the year, especially for back of house and front of house to coexist in one home. We usually rent a big home and just cook together. Last year we had Tim leading a Yoga class. And we have massages. We share common readings and reflection times. I do my cooking class. It really is about being present and intentional together. When you have that seed, it's really easy to develop at work. This restaurant is an extremely aggressive and intense environment. So for us to go into a shift feeling that you are with your team and you are with your family, I think it helps with the operation.

And now you and a friend are planning on opening a brewery?

Yes. We have been working on it for a few months now. It's still in the making process. It's an interesting journey because we have been trying to be very mindful of the reason of why we would expand. I'm trying to be intentional about that piece and if we are going to have a second space, it has to feel right in relationships first. But, yes, we are. It should be happening soon, we hope.

And why a brewery?

Expansion has never really been a part of my thinking in developing the business plan for Bida Manda. But what I have learned to embrace in life is to *pay attention with the relationships* that we have.

A friend of mine, Patrick Woodson, just moved back to town. He spent couple of years with his wife, Aubrey, in Uganda, as a Peace Corps volunteer. He has a passion for brewing, especially the Belgian style. Patrick spent some time in Laos after Peace Corps, and it was one of those moments when a lot of these stars align. I came from a culture in Laos where beer is such a meaningful craft product. Beer has such an emotional and psychological piece to the experience. In a lot of places in the world, it is about making something that is relevant to its place. And I think beer is one of those products that can nonchalantly create a community. Trophy Brewing (also in Raleigh, N.C. and co-owned by Van's mentor, Chris Powers) does a phenomenal job in challenging us and inspiring us about what a community of beer could be, just through enjoying great beer together. What we are seeking to do is allow this product to be a shared common experience. There will be a strong food component along with the beer piece.

With the level of care you put into your restaurant, does the time and focus expansion will take worry you?

Definitely. It's definitely on our mind and we have been trying to spend a lot of time reflecting on that piece. But we have to learn, and it really is about relationship building. At Bida Manda, for example, that experience is as meaningful for me as it is to a server, as it is to a bartender. I think about how we create a team that passionately cares about all these different products and experiences. They themselves become ambassadors of that narrative. I think it's unrealistic to assume that is all Van's impact. A lot of the success we see from Bida Manda is the collective effort from so many people and lives and narratives. I think as long as we continue to build communities around what we do, I don't ever foresee it to be a diluted experience.

Is there anything that has surprised you along this journey?

One of the bigger surprises, especially for me because my professional and academic journey was on such a different path than what I'm doing now, was when we decided to open the restaurant I think I felt like I was turning my back on that journey, that peace and conflict study, that community development. I developed a discomfort with that choice at the time. I have been surprised by the simple fact that it doesn't matter what discipline we find ourselves in, as long as we are true to our core beliefs and values, it's all relevant. We see Bida Manda as a community-building opportunity. How do we empower our staff in a way that they will have the courage to take on that next chapter that's meaningful to their lives? I think that was really surprising to me — that meaningful piece that this business concept yields for so many people. Because when we started, it really was a reflection, an extension of me not being able to find a job. It was a business, a professional decision. It has been rewarding to see that meaning can come out from any business journey, as long as we are *true to the things that are important to us*. And for us at Bida Manda, it's definitely community building.

Travis Todd

Ocean Odyssey

CAMBRIDGE, MD

RESTAURANT OWNER SINCE 2005

Your grandparents started a crabbing business in 1947 on the Maryland shore. Tell me about the early days and how the business has evolved into a full-service restaurant.

My grandparents started a crab processing plant down in a little hardly-known area of Maryland in Dorchester County called Crocheron. It was a very small fishing village. They set up a crab factory right around a body of water known as Fishing Bay, which is part of the Chesapeake Bay and larger tributaries. Every day, all day, they would pick crab meat and whatever fish the guys and gals out on the water brought in that day. They would go through the labor-intensive process of picking crab meat, pound-for-pound, and load that up on trucks and drive that to retail outlets, restaurants and distributors. We're talking about 1947 as far as refrigeration goes. If you look at our website, you can still see the big ol' trucks they were heaving ice blocks into the back of to keep all this seafood nice and cold. The trip to Baltimore takes an hour and fifteen minutes or so from here. But back then, trucks were a little slower, the roads were a little bit slower.

If you can imagine what was going on in 1947 and fast-forward to today (2016), you see the amount of connection to the area, to the process, to the seafood industry, to the restaurant industry. You can just imagine the amount of personal connections and stories that have developed over time, and I guess that's what fuels us to stay in this restaurant business. *It's a wild business*. But, it's neat to have those roots and that story to share for those who are willing to hear it. Sometimes, folks just want to come in and eat a fish and chips in a hurry and eat and go on about their day. We're certainly happy to provide that as well.

As your business has evolved, what are some of the values that have not changed?

First and foremost, the thing that hasn't changed is just a *feeling of belonging*, to a certain extent, and family dedication. When I say family, I'm talking about extended family as well. I think Dorchester County is truly an area where, when you hear people say it takes a village to raise a person, you know that's very much alive here. One of the things that attracted me into it is just that really strong sense of community and really strong family pride in what we do and what we enjoyed for several years throughout the history of it, and fought for, for several years of our history too. Once you sink your teeth into something you don't really want to walk away from it, even if the punches are coming pretty hard.

TRAVIS TODD

Number two, and this has always been consistent, is our dedication to using 100% domestic blue crab. I made my decision to really jump both feet first into this thing at a time where imported crab meat was hammering away at the market share of domestic crab meat, whether it was Maryland crabmeat, Virginia crabmeat, Carolina crabmeat, Louisiana, what have you. There was a big push in a lot of restaurants to purchase crabmeat sourced from Venezuela, Indonesia and elsewhere overseas. It was fine. There's nothing wrong with that product. But the problem for us was the marketing — people were coming to Maryland and sitting in these waterside restaurants and eating these "Maryland style" crab cakes. That was always the key word — "style." As long as you had that on your menu, you could use whatever you wanted. These guys were buying this crab meat from international providers at significantly less cost. I get it — sometimes in the restaurant business you run on tight margins. You have to do those things with various products. But, for us, we were so connected to Maryland seafood and Maryland crabmeat and having a background in manufacturing before being in the restaurant business that it really created a gigantic amount of respect for the product.

Did you ever consider using imported crabmeat?

That's one of the things where we definitely *draw a line on the sand*. There's a lot in this world that requires flexibility and openness, but that's one thing where we would sooner take crab cakes off the menu. It's too much a core of what we are, what we came from, and what the history of our family business is. That really comes from Pops. He was there for a couple years when that crab meat was really infiltrating the market. The guys would come by and bring us samples. They wouldn't last too long in here before he would politely ask them to walk back out the same door they came in. He didn't even want a can of that product to be seen in this place. I think that we've certainly drawn the line there and have never wavered from that. In all our minds, we're pretty proud about that.

What prompted you to join the business?

Maybe I originally jumped back into this business because I was just angry and I just thought the family could use some help. I had a ton of energy and thought, "Hey, maybe I can get in here at a time where the family needs it most." I figured out a little bit more about not just the restaurant side of things but the manufacturing side of things as well.

At that time the reality set in that it could be gone. It was the possibility of us just becoming a part of history, or a part of a crabmeat packing plant

122

that used to exist. That's what pushed me over the edge to get back in here and really try to start focusing and helping. I grew up in there. I was a kid running around the processing plant. I was a kid running around the restaurant and getting in everybody's way, stealing food off the line and hoping nobody saw it. Then I went off to school for several years in Virginia, studied something completely outside of the restaurant business and really loved it. Straight out of school I had to make a decision pretty quick. I had some job offers in the field that I had studied. But, there was just this overwhelming magnetism towards the family business and towards this town.

How long have you been part of the business?

I returned from school and really sank my teeth in the beginning of 2003, so this is year thirteen or so. It's been a little over a decade.

What changes have occurred since you joined?

When I originally got back, the backbone of our business was still crabmeat manufacturing, and selling steamed crabs in the restaurant as well as retail and wholesale. It just so happened that about the time I got back is when things started getting a little tough because the local harvests were down. Imported crabmeat was flooding the market. We were getting pretty close to panic mode. One of the areas in which I felt that I could be of help was in the actual operation of the restaurant portion of the business, which at that time was still very much a mom-and-pop place. You walk in, place your order at the counter, get a little table paddle with a number on it and when your food was up, we'd yell your number out or somebody would bring the food by. It was very simple. It was crab cake sandwiches and soft crab sandwiches and cheesesteak subs and things of that nature that were designed to be just quick comfort foods. People wouldn't spend much time here — it was super casual and easy going.

I felt that we had room to grow and improve. At the time I thought, "I have cooked enough through high school that I can jump in here and I can do this, and sure, I know what I'm doing." Turns out it's not that easy at all. But nonetheless, I stuck to it and I learned. I just kept trying to develop a different menu, develop a different style of service, and through the course of several years – and I'd say, even still today – we've basically converted from what was a manufacturing facility with a little sandwich shop in the front, to a sit-down, full-service, real-deal restaurant where families bring their kids and everybody in the community comes in. We've certainly learned and improved our menu over the years and we're focusing more and more on products from around this region. So we've converted a simple in-and-out sandwich place to a full sit-down restaurant with a great craft beer program and a beer garden outside.

And then not only that, but in different periods of time different family members were involved. The only reason we even had a kitchen in the first place is that when we moved here to Cambridge and opened the second crabmeat facility, and my grandmother — everybody around here knows her as Nanny — is not the type to sit still. She was highly involved up until she was 92. She was still here and involved in some way in the day-to-day process. Pops basically built her a kitchen because that's what she loved to do. She loved to cook. So he built her a professional kitchen to just tinker around in. Each year you develop or modify or adapt to change. In a way, it was Nanny's playhouse where she could just keep her mind occupied and it kept her involved in the business.

I've had two sisters and a brother who all have been involved. My older sister, Laura, is now very involved. She pretty much runs the front of the house operations now. We could just look at a timeline and talk about each year and what was going on with the business and what was going on with different parts of this family or different parts of the crew family involved. A lot can happen in three decades, let alone counting back to 1947.

What about the restaurant business was more challenging than you had anticipated?

It doesn't stop. I can only speak for myself, but I kind of always thought that I knew enough about it because I had cooked on the line while I was in high school. I had this inflated confidence that, "Hey, I'm not bad at this so I think I know what's going on here." When you come back then you're not just working weekends, you're not just working evenings, and you know that you're responsible for every product and to a certain degree every person under this roof on a day-to-day basis. And we're working with really high quality but highly perishable Maryland blue crabs. The shelf life on these things is a very narrow window. You have to be on top of it — you have to know your product flow because you can't really afford to take losses when you're talking about a $25 to $30 per pound product.

Being young and coming into it, I definitely was not as organized as I should have been. But the energy was there and the willingness was there. At that time, we were running Monday through Saturday and we were closed Sundays. My days would start at ten o'clock at the latest. If we were taking crabs that day we could be in here anywhere from six-thirty to seven in the morning and then you get that part of the day done and you run the lunch and then dinner starts up and then you're cleaning and you're the last one closing the restaurant down. So a lot of nights you're not out of here until ten o'clock, eleven o'clock. Then you're up the very next morning getting right back into it. Anybody in the restaurant business can tell you it's a non-stop grind and you *can't take your eye off the ball*, otherwise you're going to start taking losses or quality control is going to start slipping. Then there are issues like your walk-in cooler went down and you get that phone call at two in the morning that you've got to come back over, or if the crab truck that you were expecting at eight o'clock broke down so you've got to come back over at two or three in the morning. It's an around-the-clock, ever-demanding type of business.

There's a lot of follow-up that has to happen, too. You're pretty much always going forward, forward, forward, but you have to have that ability to reflect while you're moving forward so that you can improve. Our work lifestyle has adapted to the crab harvest to a certain extent. Now here in 2016 and for the past several years, we actually completely shut down in the winter which is nice. You get to recharge, and then you also get to reflect on the year. I feel like most of the improvements that we've made over the past decade have come from just random "aha!" moments in those winter months when your mind isn't going a thousand miles an hour.

What keeps you motivated and engaged?

Fortunately, I feel like there are a lot sources of good energy. The number one answer is just the connections to not only local customers, but people that travel through here. Ocean Odyssey has become this landmark, this evolving but unchanged and consistent landmark. Every year when we reopen, it's like you get this reunion with thousands of people that have been a close part of your life for as long as you can remember. It's pretty great when you can come to work and focus on just the pure work parts of it. But at any given moment, somebody's going to walk through that door and it's just going to be fantastic to see them. You just share stories and oftentimes it is a grind, but you forget when things are going right that you're even working. You're just part of a living story rather than watching the clock and saying, "Alright, I've only got to work for seven more hours and then I can go live." That charges your batteries, definitely.

I'm also fueled by the co-workers that are here with us now. For a lot of people who live in the community and kids who are in school, this is their first job. They come here and get a job bussing tables for a summer. Eight years later you're still working side-by-side with them in a completely different role and they're laughing and talking about, "Hey, I remember this, and I remember that." You develop these real relationships with people within your community. This year we had somebody whose great-great grandmother used to pick crabs down in the Crocheron factory. And then here they are today.

We just had our thirtieth anniversary. We threw a pretty big celebration for that. Seeing people come to that and hearing them sharing their stories and little glimpses of their life and what Ocean Odyssey's meant to them. Every time you get tired or second-guess yourself, it's a story from somebody that comes through that just *completely fills you up* with all kinds of reasons to keep on keeping at it.

What's different about the workforce today compared to a decade ago?

We've had wonderful people throughout the entire history. I'm a little closer with the workforce here today because I was cutting my teeth as a young, not-so-great leader in this business at the same time as some of the crew that are here today. They've helped me along the way, and now I realize how important it is for me to help them along the way too. Straight out of college I was all energy and I would try to cook a thousand miles an hour. If people could keep up I'd be like, "Wow, that person's great." But now I just see this willingness to learn, and really great leadership qualities in young crew members that have expressed their interest to grow their role within the company.

My brother used to work here in the early 2000's, and one of our first hires was a young kid who just came in to work a dishwasher station for a summer. Now he's twenty-four, twenty-five, and he developed a love for craft beer and he really got into it. My brother and I had the opportunity to mentor him once he was going through college. He was kind of down on himself because he didn't get a job right out of school and he wasn't doing what people thought he was supposed to be doing. He tried going into the insurance business and it just wasn't for him. He was just miserable, but an opportunity came up to work at a package store. Somewhere in the back of his mind he was like, "Ah, I've got a college degree, I can't just stock shelves." I told him, "Just go do it, because you're going to meet all kinds of industry guys." Here we are a few years later and he's a regional salesman for a distributor. He's just doing a great job. He has completely come out of his shell and it's nice to watch that happen. That kid was fourteen, fifteen years old when he first came in here washing dishes. And look at him now — he's really come into his own.

I keep referring to family but it's really true. The people you work with in this town, you're connected in so many different ways. We're here now, and we're focusing on service every afternoon, every dinner. There are all these other things happening too and the connection with all these people is just phenomenal.

Tell me about your leadership style.

The way I try to look at it is, "How can I help somebody do this task better right now? Do I need to even be involved? Do they want me to be?" It's absolutely like a coach to a certain extent. Then every once in a while, you're on the sidelines coaching and you've got to hop in based on what's happening that day. You also need to have respect for these crew members that you're working with to share the things that you didn't do well. I try to learn things like a bowling ball and just keep going. But then, share all the stories of, "Hey, don't do this this way" and then tell them how I messed up. And that helps. When you can tell people, "Hey, I messed this up, and used to do it this way" and you actually share that story with them, that sticks. They realize, "Hey, this person's *trying to help me develop*, not just bossing me around and telling me what to do."

The stories of what has worked and what hasn't worked has been a big thing for developing systems when we break down the week. It's, "This is what has to happen every Monday, this is what has to happen every Tuesday." And not only that, but, "Let's break down our ordering days. Let's break down our prep days." We used to be very reactionary. We would just come in and get fully prepared. We had no idea what we were getting fully prepared for but we would be fully prepared. We would just remain in this mental state of preparedness. By eight or nine o'clock at night, we were just burnt out beyond belief because we didn't know what to expect. So we've really tried to hone in and know our targets a lot better, and try to anticipate the flow of the restaurant on a week-to-week basis.

In Dorchester County, which is a phenomenal area, there are definitely spikes of population and tourism during the summer months. The way we operate in April versus August versus November are three entirely different ballgames. We have to adapt our methods throughout the year. It's really tricky to teach people that this is what we have to do. *Systems are absolutely pertinent* for having fresh perishable product. We create systems that allow us to serve them at their best and to not take losses by over-ordering or preparing them incorrectly.

Over the last few years you've been using more local providers. Are customers more attuned to where their food is coming from these days?

Since we were a manufacturer before we were a restaurant, the appreciation for the product was instilled in us. The customer base really enjoys that. And we've tried to communicate that more on our menu. We're proud of it, so we wanted people to know about it as soon as they sat down without hitting them over the head with it. We don't name every single thing on the menu, per se, but if anybody's interested in knowing more about it we're certainly happy to talk about it. Oftentimes a lot of the providers we're getting products from are in the restaurant with people. On our thirtieth anniversary somebody came up and said, "Oh, I really enjoyed that food," and literally the farmer was next to them in line. Right there you can introduce somebody and you're getting information right from the horse's mouth. There's definitely an awareness and certainly a curiosity for people about what are they eating and why. I think that's great.

What makes it hard to be successful in the business?

There's a lot to consider, and it can change drastically based on what part of the country or state you're in, the population size and all that fun stuff. The fact is there's always room for a great product. I don't think a lot of people necessarily are aware of how much it costs to run a restaurant. Having the parking lot packed on the weekends is a great and necessary thing, but *if the clock is ticking there's an expense happening* whether you like it or not. It's truly a business where almost every sector of the business is related to it. There's the finance part of it, there's the technology part of it, there's the labor market part of it, there's the understanding of law part of it, agriculture, you name it. Every sector of commerce and of business is connected somehow within the restaurant business. It's a whole lot more than just saying, "Hey, I've got these great recipes, let's get this thing going."

On top of that is understanding that it's really not just starting a business. If you're getting into the restaurant business, you're starting a whole new lifestyle. I don't really know if you can avoid that, because it really is. It's a non-stop, everyday commitment. It can be a great one — don't get me wrong. It can be amazing. But if you haven't been involved in one before, you'll be very surprised by how your time is going to be spent — every day, all day — thinking about it and figuring it out and trying to improve it and worrying about it and celebrating because of it. It's not really a business. If you're in it, it's a lifestyle. It can be a great one, but it is one of the biggest commitments you'll ever make.

Parting thoughts?

I'm kind of a head-down people and working mentality kind of guy. I really have appreciated the content that you guys have put up there, not only in your book but the blogs and I just enjoy your philosophy. I also know that sometimes restaurant folks don't always necessarily want to talk to people. And you get some great interviews. You provide a service to this industry that is A) very helpful, but then B) the respect you treat your customers with really resonated with me. Keep on doing what you're doing, because it's helpful. I've gotten on there and had some "aha!" moments through your blogs and interviews. So, I appreciate what you all do.

Thank you. We're lucky to have the opportunity to learn from folks like you.

Lisa Siegel

The Riverside Market & Cafe
Craft Beer Cartel

THREE LOCATIONS ACROSS TWO CONCEPTS - FORT
LAUDERDALE, FL

RESTAURANT OWNER SINCE 2008

What prompted you and your husband to start Riverside Market & Cafe?

Neither one of us were in the restaurant business. I was a school teacher and Julian was a developer. We bought some properties in the neighborhood that we lived in because we wanted the neighborhood to be better. It was one of those neighborhoods that was a little bit on the fringe. We wanted to get rid of some that element. We ended up buying the two convenience stores that were in the neighborhood that brought in that bad element, like drugs and all different kinds of things. We put some high-end items in there, some craft beer — some things that we wanted as a young couple with a young family. Then 2007 hit, and we got crushed financially with the real estate burst. We had two commercial buildings in a residential neighborhood that was almost gentrified.

That led to the birth of Riverside Market, because we couldn't go into competition with our tenants who leased the convenience store. We had to do something new and innovative. We had all the cooler doors and we said, "We love craft beer, we love wine, we love great food. Let's put together a menu of things that we love, because we can't go out to restaurants anymore, having two toddlers. Let's make a place for all of our friends to come and hang out and buy some good beer and have pizza, let the kids run around and play and see what happens." That is how Riverside Market started.

It has definitely evolved from where it first started to where it is now. We never had the expectation for it to turn into what it has turned into — that I would quit teaching and be full time at Riverside and that we would have a second location and be opening our third location or to be the first craft beer bar in Ft. Lauderdale. That was never anticipated.

How many types of craft beer do you have there?

When we first started, we had a hundred. We had ten cooler doors, so we were trying to fill up the cooler doors. No one wants to see empty cooler doors — it looks like a business that's going out of business. At first, we had a hundred beers and then we had a bunch of specialty sodas and waters. We took an ad out – the one and only time we ever took an ad out. It said we had three hundred and fifty different beers from around the world. Being that that went into print, we ordered three hundred and fifty beers from all over the world (laughs). That was really what pushed us into just going crazy with beer. Now we have six hundred and fifty different beers and about seventeen coolers and thirty-two on draft.

When I visited three years ago you had an honor system where people can grab beer from a cooler and then tell a server or the cashier how many they took. Do you still do that?

We have continued to do that. People still tell us that we're insane and how it shouldn't work because we must have all of this loss and breakage. That's really just not true. I would say it's a minimal amount of bottles that maybe don't get paid for. It's not so extraordinary that we even feel it. *When you put out into the world that you trust someone, they want to continue having that trust.*

We have the empty six-pack holders, so if a server sees four beers on your table she's going to go over and give you one of those empty six-pack holders and put them in there. No one wants to be fumbling with all these empty bottles walking through the restaurant. We still fill up those empty six-pack bottles and you bring them up to the front, and that's how we cash out. We're still doing it that way.

In addition to tables you also have couches and recliners in the middle of the space, in a prime area, which create a really inviting area. What prompted you to create this layout?

Every time I think that my husband Julian could not jam another piece of equipment, another chair or another cooler into Riverside, he miraculously moves things around and he does. It started when I was away one summer with our kids and Julian was spending so much time there. Someone said, "You know, you almost live here. You should put your couches in." Our good friend, Charles Trainor from *The Miami Herald* who's a regular, said, "We should really get some couches in here since we're hanging out in here all the time." They went to my house and they took the couches out of my living room, and brought them over to the restaurant. They rearranged the tables so the couches fit in. Julian said, "I took the couches out of the house." I thought he was joking. And I came home with the kids, and there were no couches in the house! I said, "Where are the couches?" and he said, "I told you. I took them to the restaurant."

It worked. What's funny is *we still don't have TVs*. We have these couches but we don't have TVs. We didn't really want TVs because we wanted people to talk to each other. You're on the honor system, so if you walk in and no one's coming and asking you what kind of drink you want, it leads to a conversation. You have to talk about the beer. You have to talk about the hundred sodas that we have. You have to give recommendations on things. It leads to a lot of interaction between the people who work at Riverside and the people who are coming to Riverside. A lot of times what happens is the customers who have been there before, because it's all word-of-mouth, say, "Well, this is how it works." Sometimes we'll just sit there and listen to people and we're like, "You're hired. Come join our team." They do a really great job of explaining what the process is, because it is unusual. They're used to someone bringing them their drink. But at Riverside you've got to go pick your drink, and you're looking at those six hundred and fifty different labels and you're going, "Well, I don't know. I like an IPA, or I really like a fruity beer, or I want to drink something local." You have to have a conversation, which is essential.

Your location is in the middle of a residential area with no other businesses around. It's not easy to find, but it's always busy and full of customers. It's really a destination, isn't it?

Yeah. I attribute a lot of that to Yelp and Google reviews and Facebook – a lot of social media. It's amazing to me with technology how people are finding us. Some guy came in the other day from New Zealand, and he walked in with his luggage and everything. He was here for the boat show and I'm like, "How did you even find us?" He's like, "Oh, Yelp." I was like, "Of course!"

It is in the middle of a neighborhood and originally was an old convenience store. The building was built back in the 1940's, before we had big grocery stores. It was your mom and pop market. We wanted to bring it back to that community-centric type of place, like in the fifties when you'd go pick up your milk and you'd meet your neighbors and just talk and catch up on the daily news. I believe that we really have brought it back to that.

How have you managed to maintain your atmosphere of unique hospitality with the opening of Craft Beer Cartel and more Riverside locations?

I use my Schedulefly videos that you guys made as an introduction for people to understand when they start working with us. I make them watch all of the whole series, even the "B" stuff that got cut. I was watching the video the other day where Julian was talking about how we're looking for another location. I was watching the whole thing and I just chuckled to myself to think that was only three or four short years ago. Now we have two more locations and are opening up another one. *We do what feels right for us.*

We were looking and looking and looking, and driving around and trying to find another location. With the first one it was really organic because we wanted to just make our neighborhood better. Finding another location was difficult because it didn't have that connection to who we were and where we lived. Then there was this guy, our kids played soccer together on the city league at different soccer parks, and he says to us, "I have this building that has a restaurant in it that's going out of business. You guys should really come in and take it over, turnkey." It was totally off the beaten path, in the middle of nowhere. And we were like, "This is perfect!" It's just like the original Riverside, except it's not in a neighborhood — it's in this industrial area. So this fell into our laps. We didn't have to build anything out. We were like, "This is it. This is the location. This is the second location."

We went ahead and opened up Riverside Market South, which is right here by the airport. It really is in the middle of nowhere. It's doing great. Because it was a restaurant and not a convenience store it doesn't have as many coolers, but we still have three hundred and fifty beers. I just got Julian to move a couch in. I was so excited. Someone was moving and they're like, "Hey, we have a couch for you." I was like, "Perfect! Let's put it in South." South is exciting because it has a real kitchen. It was a big restaurant, so we were able to expand our menu. We don't even have a cooktop at regular Riverside – we do mostly sandwiches, pizzas and stuff in the fryer. But now we have grill and do burgers, shrimp po'boys – we've really expanded our menu.

One of the things that I've found which hurt us and helped us was that because it was the same name and it wasn't exactly the same, people were kind of like, "Well, it's not the same as the first one." And no, it's not the same as the first one. That was a big lesson to me. If you're not going make it **exactly the same**, then people get pissed. They're like, "It's not exactly the same." Well, no, it's not. It has better food. We have burgers here and we have a much more extensive menu. We have a full-on bar here with fifty drafts. It's different than the OG, we call it, the original Riverside. It's taken on its own life form, the South location.

It's been open approximately a year. I work at a summer camp and I was away for the summer. We had finished painting and they got all the new draft lines in but we hadn't even hired anyone in the kitchen yet. Someone knocked on the door and said, "Hey, are you open?" Julian was like, "Well, our kitchen isn't open yet, but we have cold beer." We had all the coolers in and all the inventory in and all that stuff was all set up. So, he said, "Sure." And he takes a picture of the guy drinking the first beer at

Riverside Market South. Somehow, because of social media, the *Village Voice* and *The Sunset* see the picture of the guy drinking the beer at Riverside Market. Julian had written something that was like, "We don't need any big grand openings — sometimes you just open your doors and you're there." The newspapers both picked it up and droves and droves of people started coming in to see Riverside South. We had no staff there. The kitchen wasn't open. Julian was bringing potato chips and having sandwiches and pizzas and stuff delivered from the original Riverside. When I got home I was like, "Are you crazy? What are you doing? We've got to hire a full staff. You can't do it like this." It was definitely a little bit of a lesson. We couldn't do it the way we did the first Riverside, which was a very long, slow process and just neighborhood people. All of that was a big learning experience.

Craft Beer Cartel is across the street from the original Riverside. Tell me about it...

It's in the other building we own that also had been a convenience store. Before we opened the second restaurant, we opened Cartel. Originally, we wanted to combine all of this land and sell this big property to some townhouse developer because that's the business that Julian was in before the restaurant business. With the crash we ended up with these two buildings and had to do something, so we just did what we did. Maybe six years into Riverside being open, our tenant, who had a convenience store in which you could buy toilet paper, bread, laundry soap and all that stuff, decided that he wasn't going to renew his lease. Or we decided that he wasn't going to renew his lease. It was a mutual understanding. And we were like, we have this building now. We have this huge craft beer following. Riverside has gotten so busy that we can't have birthday parties in here anymore. We were doing a lot of Beer 101 and teaching about beer and teaching about different styles of beer. We had Julian's Beer Academy. And we couldn't do those things anymore because it was always loud, and there's was always a lot of people at Riverside. So we were like, "Well, let's take the convenience store back and do all craft beer."

One of the other problems that we had was because with all the coolers, people just wanted to sometimes come in and buy beer to go, which was fine — we could do that because we have a dual license. However, it made it really hard on our POS system and the people who were working in the front because you can't charge the same retail price if you are charging someone who's taking that to go out on their boat or go out to some event or go to a football game or whatever. So, we decided to make things easier on ourselves and also have a venue to do our beer classes and events and meet the brewer. Because beer is a culture. People who brew beer and own breweries are like rock stars. People want to meet them, they want to shake their hand, they want to hear their story, because they're really just normal, average people like us who love craft beer and love the craft that they're in and they have a story to tell.

Now we have a venue for our classes, our "Meet the Brewer." You can buy beer six-packs to go. We are the only home brew store in Broward County, so we have all the home brew equipment. You can come in and learn how to make beer, buy the grains and the yeast and the hops and go home and make your own beer. Every quarter we have a home brew competition where our people come in and bring the beer that they made and sample it out to people. And they get feedback. So, that's become a really fun venue and to-go store.

You're certainly staying busy. Do you still love it as much as always?

We just went through a big transition at Riverside South. We had some management changes and because we're owner-operators, we can't just throw somebody in there and say, "Okay, you're the person that's going to go in." So, Julian and I have been working a lot since the season has kicked off. Julian was opening the store and getting back to where we were seven years ago when he was opening the store every day at regular Riverside. It's a little bit humbling and it's a lot of work. One of my kids said the other day, *"Mom, I don't even know what Dad's wearing today because I never see him anymore."* Those are growing pains. It's part of that growing process, and we have to love it and accept it because that's where we are right now. It's just what has to be done. We're still doing a lot of things ourselves. Yesterday we ran out of pizza cheese. The good thing about it was that Restaurant Depot was closed, but we could run to store #2 and go grab the extra cheese that they had so we could keep on making pizza last night. It's just part of those growing pains.

It is hard, but it makes you appreciate everything so much more. You just have to look at it and say, "Yeah, this is a really hard thing and I'm running from store to store, turning keys and opening and doing this. But, I so appreciate this because it means that we're growing and, that we have a vibrant business that's working." We always take a Christmas picture, starting with four employees seven years ago. Now we have over sixty employees which is pretty amazing.

Since you run your business a bit unconventionally, you've had a lot of people tell you that you've got to change. How have you been able to say, "Thanks, but no thanks?"

We love the feedback. There are things that we're not willing to change, but then there are some things that we say, "Hey, you know what? They've got something there. And maybe, we should look at that." Especially because we're such a community-based business, we appreciate when people offer input. We have to explain the TV thing to them. When we bought South there were a lot of TVs. People are like, "Hey, can you turn on the game?" We're like, "The TVs aren't hooked up." And they're like, "Well, why do you have all these TVs here?" I'm like, "When they gave us the keys to the restaurant, the TVs were in here already. So, we just didn't take them down." But we are always willing to take people's opinions and feedback because it is important. We see whether if it's worthwhile for us or not. We appreciate it. But we're still doing it the way we were doing it."

I'll give you an example of a suggestion someone made to us. It's something that I knew that I had to do or we had to get there, especially with multiple locations. Every time we design a T-shirt for sale, I always design it in the mind that I want it for my staff because we don't have uniforms. Our uniform is a Riverside T-shirt, but anyone can have a Riverside T-shirt because we sell them. When we're really busy you don't know sometimes who works there and who doesn't. Someone recently was like, "With both locations, you really should do some branding, and have a uniform so people know who works here. Maybe it's just like your regular shirt that you do and it says 'Staff' or 'Crew' or 'Riverside Family' or something on it." That's the perfect example of a suggestion that I was like, "Yes, I know that we have to do this." That's something that we're working on right now. I was happy for that feedback.

What's been the biggest surprise since you got into the restaurant business?

The biggest surprise and the biggest blessing was when we opened South that people were so discerning. They just felt so much more allegiance and more comfortable at the original, and weren't as open to the new store. It just didn't feel as homey to them and they liked the original one more. That was a huge surprise.

It's a little bit more comfortable and set up more like a restaurant. It has a bar and the coolers, and now it has the couches and the tables and it's just a little bit more like a traditional restaurant than the original one. The great thing about that is now that we're opening up our third location, I'm taking the best parts of original Riverside and the best parts of the South location, which has this gigantic bar, and putting them together. Our Plantation location is basically the lessons that we've had in the last seven years and it's going into one store. I really feel that our new Plantation location is going to be the most successful out of all of them because it takes the best out of both restaurants that we have open now.

When is that opening?

We're crossing our fingers that it will happen before the new year.

How far away is that from original Riverside?

About five miles. It's really close, but it's in the town over so it's to the west of us. It's a little bit more suburban. People in the suburbs don't want to go to those commercial restaurants all the time, those chains. We're really excited about that. And again, it's an off-the-beaten path location – it's not on the main street. It's back in a neighborhood and it was a convenience store. I think that's become our model. We find a lot of success in these old convenience stores that bring bad elements into the neighborhood, and make them into these upscale craft beer hangouts.

We're in the midst of opening up a brewery as well, so we've got a lot going on. It's really exciting.

When is that going to happen?

We just finished our plans and the Plantation location kind of happened simultaneously. We've been approved for a site location by the city. We have the building. We do things unconventionally. Maybe that should be our tagline. We bought the equipment first. Then we found the building. Then we got approval from the city. We just finished all of our mechanical plans. Now we're going forward with a partnership and so we're ready as soon as it happens. Our plans will actually go in this week to the City of Ft. Lauderdale. Our plans are finished but we're interviewing general contractors. We just do everything backwards, but it works for us.

Do you have investors involved now?

With the brewery we're going to have an investor, which is a whole new thing for us. Someone was telling us we have to scrub the numbers because when you're going to investors they want to see spreadsheets. They love spreadsheets. So that's been a new thing for us too.

With investors, you have to find someone that understands the unconventionality of who we are. They very quickly have said, "We don't understand anything that you do but we know that it works. And we know that you're going to make it work." It's that sink-or-swim kind of philosophy. You want to go hard or go home, so we're just going for it.

Any last thoughts?

Justin is running South now. When we first started Justin lived in the neighborhood near Riverside. Because we only had three or four employees, when we would get really busy Julian would go run over to Justin's house and bang on the door and say, "Justin, we need help. We're really busy. Come to work. Get dressed, I'll drive you over." Now because of Schedulefly, Justin knew that he had to open this morning. People used to write down their hours of when they used to work. Now we feel super-organized because we can look at our sheets for our employment, see what our labor costs are, when we're busy, and when we need to cut people. We are looking at those things and you guys are a huge part of that.

We could not be where we are today without you. I feel like I always say you're like our Riverside cousins, because we think of ourselves as a family. There is no way we could possibly be where we are today – with the amount of employees that we have, all of the different locations, knowing where we're supposed to be when — if it wasn't for you guys. So, I thank you very much for being there.

Sean Degnan

bu•ku

so•ca

TWO LOCATIONS ACROSS TWO CONCEPTS -
RALEIGH, NC

RESTAURANT OWNER SINCE 2010

Tell me about your background in the restaurant industry.

My partner Tony and I worked for Rocky Top Hospitality for a long time and we opened a lot of restaurants for that company and then decided to go out on our own. We met up with William D'Auvray of Fins Restaurant, which was in north Raleigh for a long time, and it was a really awesome little restaurant. It moved downtime right when the economy crashed. So there was this beautiful, fine-dining seafood restaurant in downtown Raleigh and it needed some new life. We came up with a small plates street food concept that we thought would be a little more fun, a little more inviting. It's a place that you could go a couple times a week instead of a couple times a year for your birthday or your anniversary. We came up with a menu that was street food from all over the world that's fun to talk about, fun to learn about, and fun to drink alongside.

So you and Tony had worked together for a long time?

We worked together at seven different restaurants. We started together at Michael Dean's, and then we opened up Bogart's and High Fives and The Red Room and Twisted Fork and by the time that I left Rocky Top, I was director of operations and Tony was kind of becoming the director of culinary. We were talking to some other people about opening our own place and just kind of got that ball rolling.

Knowing that it's a tough business, what made you want to make that leap and take on more responsibility and risk?

Survival and the need to make money is part of it. But, we also loved it. We really love working together. When we started coming up with concepts together, we were working as chef and sous chef, prepping side-by-side all day, listening to loud music. We were just talking about if it was ours what would we do differently. That was when we were working at The Red Room and it was small plates and tapas, when tapas were very new to Raleigh. People that called on the phone would say "Are you topless? Or topaz?" We're like, "No, we're tapas" (laughs). It was just a fun and exciting time. Food was getting really exciting in Raleigh. We just kept coming up with different ideas, and when we went and looked at different spaces, we came up with different concepts. When we met William, who had had an amazing restaurant for years and years and years, it was fun to sit down with him and come up with something that was totally different than anything anyone had seen around here.

Three partners. Tell me about that...

The scariest thing is trusting that the other person is not going to walk away when it gets really tough. We've had been in nearly knock-down, drag-out fights out back, away from everybody else, disagreeing about something that we thought really important at the time. It's like a marriage. But people get divorced all the time, so in some ways it's more than a marriage. You know that no matter what is said or how bad the night goes that you're going to be working together tomorrow so you might as well come to some sort of realization together that you're going to have to be able to get through this.

We had been through some tough times together. There were just nights that didn't go right. There was a night that we actually moved Tony into his new house and we had a new sous chef at the Red Room, and it was Sunday night when we did this all-you-could-eat tapas buffet. We came in and our new sous chef had been watching football all day long and he wasn't ready at all. We came in and it was a disaster. But even after nights like that, the fact that you *know that person's not going to walk away*, it makes it so that you can have a real fight, so that you can say everything that's on your mind and the next day they're still going to be there. That's really important.

You and Tony had a history together, but you didn't know William. How do you bring somebody new into the fold and make that work?

We weren't very successful with it. William was with us for about a year of planning at bu•ku, but he was going through some personal tough times and had a divorce so he actually moved on a little bit later. But, he definitely helped us. He was the brainchild of a lot of the menu to start with. He was an awesome partner to have for as long as we had him. He has a restaurant in Portland, Maine now.

We have brought on a lot of people that are definitely like family to us. In fact, members of our family worked with us on and off in the restaurant. We're able to bring people on and create those relationships. But I don't think any of the relationships are as strong as the one we have because the two of us can't leave. Everyone else can quit and go on about their lives, but the two of us will be there till the doors close.

Your wife, Mandy, is involved in the business as well.

Yep. She's seven months' pregnant right now, so she'll be taking a little break here in a couple months. Tony's wife, Ellen, also worked to help open the restaurant, too, until she had their first child. She was our events coordinator and our hiring manager. Mandy kind of took over her role. Mandy was the bar manager and she took over Ellen's role after Ellen went on maternity leave. But, Mandy and I have worked together for most of the time that we've known each other. So it was actually harder for us when we worked in different restaurants which is weird, and very unlike most relationships. It'll actually be weird and different for us when we don't work together, when she has the baby.

How did you come up with the "global street food" concept?

We wanted something that was great food but wasn't necessarily super expensive food and it had a great story and a great history. We kind of went to not necessarily classically-trained chefs in our kitchen, but we have great people in our kitchen. They're from Colombia and Mexico and they all had their own recipes. Our Arepas, our Empanadas, we had a chef that made amazing Ceviches and Teritos from Peru, we just kind of took all those things that everyone grew up cooking. Tony had traveled. William grew up on the west coast and came up in sushi restaurants. Andrew Smith, who as our sous chef and is now chef-de-cuisine had traveled Southeast Asia, too, so we kind of leaned on all these people. Then it just becomes exciting because you can study and learn all kinds of different cuisine and add it to the menu. There are a ton of different influences, and then we also went out and learned some on our own.

What do you do really well that helps make bu•ku so successful?

Sometimes *being lucky is just as good as doing a good job*. Downtown Raleigh is really taking off. Ashley Christensen being here helps a lot. The fact that the Red Hat (a very large publicly traded software business) moved into our building — that was huge. It was a Progress Energy building and then Red Hat took it over. That's a young, hip, fun company to work for. Having those guys as our lunch guests and happy hour crowd — that's pretty great.

And we've tried to respond to all the feedback we've gotten over the years. When we started we were closed on Sunday. Now we do this crazy huge brunch on Sundays, because it seemed like something that people wanted. We used to be open until two in the morning. We thought that we'd just be open until two and have live music and DJs — we thought that was really important for downtown Raleigh. Then all these great bars sprung up around us. We get to close at ten during the week and midnight on the weekend, and people just go from our place and go hang out at these other great bars that we also like to go to.

We try to respond to everybody. We have valet set up every night, so people who are afraid to park downtown and think that downtown's such a difficult place to get around — we try to appeal to those people, too. We just take the feedback. We've been humbled many times with people's suggestions. We have ten managers who sit down every Monday and we go over all the problems of the week, and try to fix them.

How do you draw the line between somebody being unreasonable and somebody having a legitimate complaint?

If you think about it, nobody's coming out trying to have a bad time. We're really lucky to have guests that are there to try new food. They're almost always celebrating something or going out somewhere to an important show. So, we start off with this great clientele. They're just trying to try out some new stuff. If they're trying out something that just doesn't sit well with them, then you have to accept that and they're probably not trying to do anything malicious when they complain — they're probably just offering good, constructive feedback. Sometimes the way that we want it presented or the way that we want to cook something is not necessarily the way that they think it should be. We take it all in.

Think about barbecue in North Carolina — everyone has a different opinion of what barbecue in North Carolina should taste like. So, think about that when you're presenting empanadas, which are from South and Central America. If someone who's been traveling through Central America and South America tastes your empanada and says, "This is nothing like what an empanada is supposed to taste like," you have to just understand they've tasted the real thing. They're going to be different. Our interpretation is going to be different than theirs, and hopefully we put enough time and effort and research into it that it seems like we presented the most authentic thing that we can. But, people's opinions matter a lot to us. And, we're tweaking the recipes every week.

We're just really lucky. We're lucky to have the guests that we have, we're lucky to have the staff that we have. The fact that we get to do what we love every day is really important. There's some people around us doing it as good or better than we are. So, we have something to strive for. If you have ever been to Bida Manda, that's probably one of the most hospitable places to eat in downtown Raleigh. Van Nolintha and his sister Vanvisa do an amazing job of making you feel at home. I think about that every time when I go to work, how comfortable he makes me feel when I sit down in his restaurant. It's something to shoot for and it's admirable.

How have you been able to find people who truly believe in what you're doing?

That's something we really had to stop and think about. When we opened, just like any other restaurant, you have to hire on so many people, and you lose people. At a certain point, it becomes frustrating to hire somebody, believe in them, train them, and then for whatever reason in a short amount of time they leave. It just seems after a while the people that are training them, the people that are putting in this extra work, they get a little discouraged. So we had to really stop and say, "Okay, we're going to take this seriously *every single time*."

When we interview somebody it's me and another manager asking, "Why do you really want to do this? What do you love about serving people? What do you love about food and drink? When you go out to eat, what's your favorite thing? What's your favorite restaurant? What do you like to drink?" We start a conversation about why they really want the job. When you feel like you're bringing on someone that you really want to work with, somebody you want to be there with, day-in and day-out, hanging out, joking around, then that's a good candidate. Then you put your heart and soul into teaching them everything that you know.

It starts with taking the hiring process really seriously and not just taking everybody that seems like they might be a good fit. Then it's sticking with them. We still lose good people that we would have liked to have kept for a long time. It's a college town and we're lucky to have all these really smart and exciting people that maybe the restaurant industry isn't their dream. So they do this for the three or four years while they're in college. It's really awesome to have that group of people to work with. But then you get to see them go on about their careers and you wish them the best.

Mostly, we try to have fun together at work. We have a lot of programs in place at work that remind us that what we're doing is fun and not just like the daily grind of working in a cubicle. We literally have a gold star chart where we focus on positive things and put up gold stars when people go out of their way, or they pick up a shift for somebody who's sick, or they just go above and beyond. At the end of the month whoever has the most gold stars wins a hundred bucks. We have a sales goal for the night — it's based on last year, or it's based on the reservations. When we hit that number, everyone gets a free beer after work. We close down for company parties. We do a baseball/kickball game, and company cookout on Memorial Day. We do a Super Bowl party. We just try to do as many things to take care of the good people that really enjoy working together every day as possible. When you lose good people it hurts. But, at least you know you gave it a good try.

How did you finance your business?

We put in our own money, and then we had some friends put in some money. We made it so that they got paid back first, so that we didn't feel like we were putting them out. They got paid back in a little over a year. They would be excited to do something else with us again, in the near future, which we might do. After five years, we might be at the point where we've either forgotten how hard it was to open it up in the first place, or we're just that comfortable with our staff and we have a lot of great talent that would like to try something else.

How did you structure it?

You can do it straight as a loan, or you can do it as a percentage. If you're doing a percentage, the smartest way to do it is to have your investors own a greater percentage before they get their original investment back, then when they get that back, they go down to a smaller percentage.

What have you learned from somebody you admire and what do you hope people learn from you?

Ashley Christensen is a pretty popular figure for everyone thinking about food in Raleigh. I think the most important thing she does is that she always *keeps the focus on Raleigh*. She's really happy that Raleigh is emerging as a culinary destination. She points to everyone else's successes right alongside with hers. She points out other chefs that are deserving. It's really nice to see that from someone who's obviously earned a lot of success and she gives back. Some people think that they want that kind of fame. But most of the time, when I see her, she's working at a charity event of some sort. That takes up a lot of time.

And for me? I don't know. I have a fifteen-year-old son. If I can keep him on the straight and narrow, that's enough for me.

Are there any commonalities you see in restaurants that don't make it?

Hubris is probably the worst thing — thinking you know everything, and *not taking advice*. Not listening, not having respect for the authorities. I've seen people not take health inspections seriously. I've seen people not take the opening inspections seriously, thinking that they know it all. They don't take feedback from guests seriously. Then when they close their doors, they're, like, "What happened?" If you think that you know everything there is to know about anything — especially about food because it's always changing — you're wrong. You could turn on the TV and learn about ten different cultures and food that you've never seen or understood before. So if you're walking into it thinking that you're the best, you'll be humbled very quickly. That's just it. Don't think you know everything. And just listen to people. They're probably just trying to help you out.

Parting thoughts?

Definitely surround yourself with some smart people to take care of the things that you're not good at. If you're good at making really amazing food and giving great service, and you're not a lawyer, then get a good lawyer. Get a good accountant. Have those people take care of the things that you're not the best at. But, obviously, you have to pay attention to it and you can't be blind to it. Try to go into business with people that you trust and you have a good relationship with. Before the building was Red Hat, it was Progress Energy. They really did everything they could when they were building Fins for William to try to make him successful. They couldn't have predicted that the economy would do what it would do. But, when Red Hat came in, they've been really, really helpful to just to try to make us successful. So, get in with a good group of people that you trust, that are interested in your success. Red Hat wants to have a great restaurant downstairs for their employees. They do whatever they can to help us. And, obviously, when they do their Christmas parties or their after-work end-of-quarter parties, we throw down for them and they throw really good parties and we're there to help them do that. I really just suggest working with good people who you trust and who are interested in your success.

Leroy Fox

Cowbell Burger & Whiskey Bar

Mortimer's Cafe & Pub

THREE LOCATIONS ACROSS THREE CONCEPTS –
CHARLOTTE, NC

RESTAURANT OWNER SINCE 2010

How did you get started in the restaurant business?

My third-grade teacher told me if I ever needed a job to call her. When I was 14 years old I took her up on her offer. Her husband owned a very successful restaurant that was attached to Southpark Mall called Charley's. It was there for a long, long time. They hired me as a dishwasher, and I worked there for nine years. I worked up through the kitchen and ran every position there except for the center of the line. I then got into the front of the house and bussed tables, waited tables, bar backed and bartended. They were really excellent operators that had a great philosophy on taking care of their staff. They taught me everything they could about the restaurant business. I graduated from college with an accounting degree and got out of the restaurant business and told myself I would never go back.

Why was that?

It's a challenging business. The majority of restaurants are open seven days a week. You are either in the store or responsible for staff, depending on the business model, for approximately 19 to 20 hours a day, seven days a week. Our first employees are in at seven-thirty in the morning, and most nights we have the last people leaving between two and three-thirty a.m. It's a *lot of hours to be responsible for people*. It's a lot of days to handle issues and you go the entire year, usually the most busy on holidays while everyone else is on vacation. It's not a traditional job where you put your hours in and you get to go home to your family and spend nice quiet nights and weekends at home doing things with them. It's an every day, all day venture.

What brought you back to the restaurant business?

We started developing real estate and deploying money in equities after I graduated from college. There was a guy who lived in the same high rise my wife and I lived in who was also a tenant at a property that I managed — the Epicentre — in the Great Recession. He got into some financial trouble. He was a full-time sales rep with a great salary but started building custom homes on the side. He was also the franchisee of a small coffee shop. He had an interesting business model — it was a coffee shop during the day and then he'd try to turn it into a lounge at night to drive revenue later in the day when coffee sales take a massive decline. I think it was just confusing for the consumer. My wife was talking to him one day and got word that he had a cash flow problem with this coffee shop. She suggested I talk with him and see if there was something we could do to help him avoid filing for bankruptcy. So, we went in there and took a look at the financials and the issues. With everything I knew about business and everything I knew about restaurants, I told myself that it seemed almost impossible to lose money if we tried this venture. We put a team together and we took it over. We closed on January first in 2009, and the rest is history. Funny thing about life is that you never know when skills you have the opportunity to acquire if you put in the effort can be applied later in life and really provide you with an edge. Specifically, when I was employed as a kid I could have treated that job like some terrible $4.50 an hour job that wasn't worth making any effort to try to master. But I was not raised in a family that accepted a mediocre outcome from any task. We were raised to do our best and to do the job right the first time. I worked very hard while I was at Charley's and in return I learned a ton of valuable lessons. Never did I anticipate that first job would have such an impact on my family's life. So, we put a team together, acquired the store and the rest is history.

And that was Mortimer's?

Yes. The retail business beside it — a sunglass store — had gone out of business, so we combined the two and we took assignment of the guy's lease. We added the square footage with the landlord and we blew the walls out. We identified the size of the coffee shop was rather problematic when you tried to get enough seats to drive sales to cover just your fixed costs. We needed the additional square footage to have a fighting chance. Sixty-seven days later we reopened under a completely new brand, new menu, new sign — we redid the entire interior, built a substantial bar and added a little bit of square footage and one additional bathroom.

You were part of the ownership group for the property, right?

Yes. I was in a partnership. I was the minority owner, a very minority owner, really just the operating partner. The two majority owners wouldn't cut us a deal for that space unless we took the deal that the tenants had negotiated. So, we ended up just stepping into the business deals that were cut by the prior tenants to get the two majority owners of the development to agree to allow us to take it over as a tenant. That was crazy, as both concepts failed and there was no rent coming in and not many people were excited about leasing space in December of 2009. But that was the deal we had to take.

Then we started working on Leroy Fox the next year, and we opened three restaurants in four years.

That's a big transition, quickly. What did you do well?

I was working in real estate and on the fund, so I think I at least had an understanding of the fundamentals of the business and the knowledge to acquire real estate that will give you a fighting chance to succeed in the restaurant game. I think that's one of the key components to success — make sure that you have a location that helps you more than hurts you. In the restaurant business, you need to have so many things going for you. The business is really fascinating. I've always been fascinated by restaurants because of the core philosophy required to succeed. You must be in the business for one reason: to serve your customers! Everything that you do while you're open should be around that central tenet that you are in the customer service business. *If you don't have a deep love for serving your customers, I don't think it's the place to be.* We really focused on the customers when we opened Mortimer's. The customers and the culture, I think, are the two most important things. I sat up for a few nights and wrote thousands of sentences that would end up be a guiding mantra for us. Early in the morning, maybe around 3am, I got it. "Working to Preserve Old Fashioned Service." I own that trademark and it is what we live by, our primary guiding principle. It is not rooted in hubris and in fact allows a lot of fallibility. Because we say "Working to…" we can in theory mess up and, so long as we fight to recover, we are still within our brand promise. Everyone that works for us believes in our mission to work to Preserve Old Fashioned Service.

We put together a collection of really great service industry people that were the difference in the success of the first restaurant. Everyone that worked for us, down to the guys or girls in the back washing dishes or cooking, to the servers, hostesses, bar tenders, busboys, to our security — they all just really cared about the customers. I think we were really fortunate to surround ourselves with some great people. To this day, I think the thing that we have been most successful at doing is hiring people that shared similar values to us. I'm sure like at every restaurant there are people that have not had great experiences at our restaurants. You can't win every time. But we go out of our way to try to make the experience a hundred percent about the customer.

Tell me about your business partners.

We have a great group of partners in our restaurants and everyone brings their unique talents to the collective table. The stores are really a reflection of all of us in some ways, but the most influential on the design & menu aesthetic is Brandon Viebrock. He and I work on the acquisition, layout, design, and construction of each store. We have made plenty of design mistakes but each store takes on a unique personality and we learn something each time. One of these days we will get one right. We have a great management team and staff that constantly strives to improve our food, operations, procurement and customer service and they are our partners too.

What is different for staff about working for your restaurants than they may have experienced at other restaurants?

One thing that we do well is that we have a group of owners and operators that generally love being around other people. These are people that are energized by being around people and they love having the opportunity to do something special that could change someone's monotonous day. As an ownership group, we recognize that the employees you hire communicate and interact more with your customers on a daily basis than you do. If you can hire a group of people that treat people similar to how you would treat them, I think you can perpetuate a culture that is about taking care of each other. I believe that we should treat our employees better than any other employer because we want to retain the best employees. We have really low turnover compared to industry averages, and we can always be better.

Danny Meyer's book, *Setting the Table*, is one of the best books about life in general. The outlook is so spot on. Everyone that works for us gets a copy, usually with a handwritten note by one of us on the ownership side or the management side. I just think it's a profound book for service industry people. *Setting the Table* has had a massive impact on our culture and me personally.

Do you have a good process for identifying people who might not be a good fit after you've hired them?

That's a classic predicament. People can interview extremely well and then, for whatever reason, can't perform up to the impeccable standard that they said that they could achieve when you interviewed them. We have the same predicament that I assume everyone has, where we feel certain we've got a great candidate, and for whatever reason it just doesn't work out. We found some great service industry people early on and we relied heavily upon recommendations from them for people that they felt were people that were like-minded or people that would fit into our culture. We found the most success with people that were referred by some of our best employees. Once we got a critical mass of great people, then it just sort of perpetuated. We've hired outside of that circle and been successful and unsuccessful for various reasons. We try to make changes very quickly when we find someone that's not up to our service standards. It's been rare that we've had those issues. We've been very fortunate.

Our customers have given us great employees over the years, especially younger kids starting as busboys or hostesses that lived in the neighborhood. When they've gotten to working age their parents wanted them to come work for us. That is very humbling and such an honor that you may have the opportunity to impact someone's life no matter what they choose to do for a profession. They're great parents with great values, and they teach their kids accountability and ethics and morals. We've been really fortunate to have people from the neighborhood want us to employ their children, who have grown up to become great employees for us.

Recently, Gary Laughlin. Both of his children worked for us and he and his wife came in every day. He was an exceptional man and everyone that came in contact with him loved him. I went to his funeral with the GM of our store. I looked around and saw maybe eight of our employees at the service. I think that says a lot about our staff. These servers and bar tenders and managers could have done anything with that afternoon but they came to support that family. I was deeply saddened by the loss of such a great husband, father and patron, but very proud of our people's priorities.

You mentioned to me once that leading by example is important to you. What's an example of you doing that?

Cowbell was previously a restaurant called Nick's Burger Bar that had gotten into some trouble. It's on the bottom floor of a high rise building in downtown Charlotte. That downtown lunch crowd is a finicky group and has a fixed window to dine in. It's kind of a kill-or-be-killed environment. The margin of error in the whole entire process is very small.

We were in there early on, before we had changed the name, and it was still Nick's Burger Bar. We kept the staff until we closed for renovations to determine who we felt could be great employees. While we were designing and planning our brand change and the close of the restaurant, I was in there trying to meet the existing customers to find out what they liked and didn't like and what their needs were so that we could build a concept out that was more in line with the customers that were already there. On this one particular day, something happened with the ketchup. The previous ownership had some rather lax practices and some of the ketchup had fermented. Per a customer's request, I delivered a bottle of ketchup to a table filled with professionals dining in their business attire. A gentleman opened the ketchup and it exploded all over him. It was not a minor incident — it was a major explosion. I can't quite fully explain how it happened or what the chemistry is behind what happened in the bottle, but it was a disaster. Not only did we have to perform and get their food out quickly, but I had a guy that I could not, in good faith, send back to work in the state he was in. While he was dining, I found out his shirt size. There was a Joseph A. Banks a couple buildings down the street. I ran down there and I bought him two different shirts — I didn't know which one was going to fit him the best. I ran them back and delivered them to him at the table. I apologized profusely and said he could keep both shirts. He was very happy with us and is still a customer. I see him in there frequently. We still laugh about that shirt incident. But I just figured it was the right thing to do. I don't think I did anything special. I just think you have a great responsibility when you're a restauranteur to serve the public, not get them sick, plate great food and obviously, if you trash someone's clothes on the shift, you can't send them back to work the rest of the day with a ketchup-laden, white button-down. I comped the whole table for everyone at the table. We make a joke in our restaurant that that's a POTUS operation. That is the President of the United States-type service interaction where *everyone immediately goes to resolve any and all ill-will for the brand*, reconciling any customer grievance prior to them leaving the four walls of our store.

How do you empower your staff to replicate that type of response?

We empower our employees to behave like we would in a situation like that. We are a hundred percent at fault for things like that. To inconvenience the customer is unacceptable. So, each employee, each manager, they can own those situations. We prefer that they own them to a resolution because we don't like to pass the buck and hope that someone resolves it. I'm sure that we have some online reviews where we didn't fully resolve a situation, but we do try to go out of our way when we can. If any employee that works for me has any situation like this, they know that if they're the one that buys that shirt that I will one hundred percent reimburse them. And I would appreciate it. If I find that they didn't go buy the shirt in a situation like that, they know that they will have some answering to do. We don't hold a different standard for ourselves than we hold for our employees. We try to put everyone in the same boat. They know that they are fully authorized to handle any customer complaint.

We prefer to go over the top to make a customer leave happy when they're unhappy, just because we think it's the right thing to do. There have been countless examples of employees of mine leaving to buy a *Wall Street Journal* for a customer who asked if we have one. We don't even have newspapers in our restaurants, but I just try to teach them to take care of it if it is not an exuberant cost or puts us in duress. You may hear someone say, "Oh, it's Janet's birthday." You don't even have to ask the table. You go in the back and make a dessert for her and come out and deliver it to her and tell her it's on us. For a little girl's birthday party one time, we overheard the parents talking about her favorite cake. We didn't sell anything like it in the restaurant. One of the employees drove down the street to a bakery and bought a fifty-dollar cake with candles and brought it back and presented it to the table. The parents were wowed. *It's little things that make them come back over and over again*. But it's also a way to make the world better. It changes the whole way they experience the day. We hope they pass along that one little bit of happiness. If we can just do general acts of kindness for people within our four walls and try to make the world a better place as a core philosophy, I think that is the type of culture that we are looking to build on for years.

You mentioned the importance of knowing when piece of real estate is going to set you up for success or when it may set you up for a struggle. What are you looking for?

Real estate is a lot like human beings. Every property has little things about it that make it unique. Obviously, the assets like location and parking and those things are massively important. That's Real Estate 101. Customer engagement in an area is also extremely important. For instance, I would think it's better for a restaurant to be around other restaurants. I think a lot of times consumers can't make a decision on what type of fare they want but they'll generally head towards an area that has a bunch of options, and just pick when they're there. If that is the area where they frequent for food, the resulting trip to that area would be dining in your restaurant one night, dining at the guy next to you the next night, and you can kind of keep them in that trip circle. Sometimes people will make a decision for real estate because their rent is lower at the expense of a lot of other very important inputs. Sometimes the most expensive rent isn't the best real estate deal either. We really like second generation restaurant space as a business philosophy. The failure rate is so high that we feel like if we can find the right space and we don't think it's a real estate problem — we think it was an operator problem or a concept problem — we feel like we can save a lot of money not having to put in air conditioning and sheet rock and electrical. We can redo the restaurant to where it is a completely different customer experience and a completely different layout. That money we try to save we can pass along to our customers on our menu pricing.

The real estate thing's tricky. It's sort of a gut instinct over doing tons of transactions that's hard to put into words. There are some buildings that I personally shy away from, for whatever the reasons are. I've seen other operators go in and become wildly successful, and then I think to myself, "Man, where did I go wrong on that one?" And then the flip side, I've shied away from some that I thought were horrendous and I've seen people go in and spend millions of dollars to make the place nice and they failed miserably. Some of it is unquantifiable. But the real estate game is location, location, location. That's what everyone talks about.

Parking and access are important too. It's *going to be interesting with Uber* as more consumers utilize that as a service. Can you be successful at deploying a restaurant in areas where the parking was a significant hurdle for the prior restaurateur? Especially with late night travel in urban areas, it might not have such a big impact anymore with this change in transportation. Does that allow some other great spaces that have generally not been great real estate spaces for restaurants change the dynamic on that? I think the jury's still out. But I do have my eye on a couple spots that I think could be great real estate if that is the truth.

You've used some creative, unconventional marketing. What's are some examples?

Two elections ago I was taking my kids to the library and I saw a slew of election signs for local candidates and national candidates, Congress, Senate, judges and sheriffs — it just dawned on me that the signage ordinance for political signs was way more lenient than temporary signs that were allowed to be put in front of the restaurant for whatever reason. There are all these regulations that you have to abide by. I Googled "Leroy Fox" to see if anyone was named Leroy Fox. I felt like the name of our restaurant was clearly in the gray. There were a couple people that had not so great records pop up in the Google search, but I thought to myself, "Perfect. This is a real person. The city can never get me on this one." We manufactured yard signs and we put them up in front of houses all over the city. The customers loved them. We made "Vote Leroy Fox" bumper stickers. We had an election party. All these parents brought their kids up. We had a little fake ballot thing at the front. It was a really great low-cost impression value campaign for us, because we had some older customers come into the restaurant and tell us, "I spent thirty minutes on the internet trying to figure out who this Leroy Fox candidate was, and then my buddy told me it was your restaurant. Now I'm here." Although I felt bad that they spent so much time on the internet in a futile pursuit, I was very happy that they made it to the end place and we got a good laugh out of it. It was a really fun campaign for us. We'll see what happens in the future but hopefully we can keep that going.

Also, at Leroy Fox, we have a magical mailbox by the hostess stand in the front of the restaurant during December. When the hostess seats a family, she will give the kids a little piece of paper for their wish list for Santa Claus. On the back, there's a funny section that has a mailing address and a box for the parents to check on whether their kid was naughty or nice. The kids fill them out and most of them don't have the best penmanship. Some of them are illegible, for sure. Some of them give me an address with no zip code.

I go in and hand write letters back to them all. You have a great responsibility when you are holding yourself out as Santa Claus to respond to these little children's letters. You have to use a feather calligraphy pen that you dip in an ink well. You have to have great stationary, and you have to have great penmanship — you *cannot* misspell the child's name. Santa Claus would never do that. You cannot reference any gifts as you could put a parent in a bad situation where they may or may not have the means to buy the gift for the child. The language in the letter has to be specific and I spend a considerable amount of time crafting these letters. I handwrite all the envelopes as that is the initial visual and I think super important for the child as the envelope usually causes them so much joy even prior to reading the letter. At one point, I took all these letters to the post office and I asked the lady if they could stamp them like in the movies where they look like they came from all over the world, and she looked at me like I was crazy and she said, "Sir, no one does that in real life. That's just in the movies." I bought all these rubber stamps, I probably had six different colors, and I stamp the envelopes like crazy to make it look like the elves stamped the envelopes.

We've done various iterations of this over the years. It is super fun. It's probably more rewarding for me than it is for the children that get the letters. It's always great to see the families come back and the parents are laughing and thanking us. We go to great lengths to make sure that the address and the zip codes are right, even when we can't read. I go to Mecklenburg County real estate to look up the address and find out the parents' names. Sometimes I've had to go to Facebook and stalk the mom to make sure I had the kid's name is spelled correctly, or I have the correct gender.

We do that more just to make the world a better place. I think we get brand equity out of it and people bring their children in every year for it so it seems to spread good cheer. It's grown every year and it's getting rather burdensome — I may need some elves to help me in the future.

If parents are having particular difficulties with their children they get custom letters trying to adjust the behavior from a Santa Claus point-of-view, on behalf of the parents. It has been rather comical to hear the stories from parents about the faces their kids made when Santa Claus called them out on a particular deficiency.

Unlike other retailers, I have a rule that the mailbox goes up the day after Thanksgiving. I think there's something super unholy about starting Christmas prior to Thanksgiving being over. So, we wait. And that day is the day that the mailbox shows up. My own kids get letters that they do believe are still from Santa Claus. And I have adjusted some behavior between my three boys with these letters that really was pretty impressive.

This really has very little to do with operating a restaurant, but it is *the little things* that make the difference.

Do you intend to continue to grow the restaurant group?

Seth, Andrew and I run a long-short equity fund during the day, which is our primary job. We've started the restaurant operation as kind of an experiment that went better than we could have ever imagined. We've continued to do them and we've worked really hard at hiring great managers and putting them together with our culture and our systems. We have great employees and managers and we would be foolish not to continue to fund them if they have the ability to continue to grow stores and profitably operate them. We want to provide as many career opportunities as we can. With that being said, we are negotiating right now for another Leroy Fox. Maybe in the next seven or eight months we'll have that store open. The good news is we're going to duplicate Leroy Fox, and hopefully take what we learned at the first one and see if *we were lucky or if we are actually good*.

Do you have any advice for people thinking about getting into the restaurant business?

The business is really about the customers. Every decision that we've made has really been about whether or not it was in the best interest of the customers. Then we just sort of manage the business result on our side afterwards. We have a core philosophy where, although we'd love to win a James Beard Award, we feel like if we plate really great food that is of considerable value to the customer for the quantity that they're getting and the price that they're paying, and we source the best ingredients that we can, that if we take care of the customer and provide exceptional service, and we're really serious about making their day a little bit better, we can be in business for a long time. Sometimes I think people get really caught on really being just about the food, and kind of going to that elitist side. It's hard because the customer expectation in that type of environment is that the food has to be perfect, and if it's not you've held yourself out to such a high standard that it's hard to manage that expectation.

We've tried the opposite. We try to over deliver from what we've promised to the customer. And we like to step over one foot hurdles versus trying to jump over a four foot ones. I don't know if there's any one model that's right or wrong. All the models are an extension of you. *If you're yourself and you really care about your customers,* I think you can do great in the business.

We've just put together a really great group of people. Some of our best ideas have come from places where you may not think you would get a great idea. Our management staff and our bartenders and our servers and our busboys and our front-of-the-house people and our back-of-the-house people and our catering manager, our marketing people — they just come to work happy every day, and they work really hard to try to make the customers have a great day. Our success one hundred percent goes back to the team. We are very blessed to have some great people.

Subculture Coffee

TWO LOCATIONS - DELRAY BEACH AND WEST
PALM BEACH, FL

RESTAURANT OWNER SINCE 2009

Tell me about the genesis of Subculture Coffee.

I've been a coffee lover for a while. I'd never worked in a coffee shop but I've played a lot of music. When you travel and you play music, you spend a lot of your downtime in coffee shops. I'd always dreamed of doing that one day when I decided it was time to settle down. About six years ago, I did a space share with my brother just to limit startup costs. He had an art gallery, so I figured it would work well if we shared space. I opened up a little coffee stand in the gallery, just me and my wife, a barebones approach, just outside of D.C. That's where it all started. That was my first coffee job. I'd never worked in coffee before I opened the shop. I don't know if that was the smartest thing, but it's worked out so far.

South Florida is what I call a wasteland of good coffee, so I figured it's a good opportunity for me because I think everyone can appreciate good coffee. They just need to be exposed to it. I think in cities where it's developed it would actually be harder to get into the market and make a living doing it, whereas down here, I figured the product would sell itself and it'd be easy to get my foot in the door with minimal cost. It was just me and my wife, the overhead was really low and we could run it super-efficient.

And that was the case. Though in the past two years, there's been quite a few other coffee shops and roasters pop up. Panther Coffee in Miami started about the same time I did down here, about three years ago, and now they're pretty big, along with a few other places. We're creeping on the scene, finally.

Tell me about roasting your own beans.

We roast all our own stuff. That was a new thing for me. I had worked with Counterculture when I first opened the coffee shop six years ago. I was a customer of theirs for about four years. We switched over to roasting our own when we rebranded as Subculture, because I teamed up with another guy here and we thought it would be a good idea to give that a go. We both really wanted to have a story from start to finish. It's kind of popular now to say direct-trade relationships. But if you're looking at a business, it's really nice to be able to know, farm-to-cup, what's going on with your product. A large part of why we started roasting was just so that we could have pretty good control and personal relationships with the people in our supply chain.

How do you find high quality beans?

It's difficult. That's definitely the hardest part. Coffee is the second-most traded commodity in the world. It's huge. There's just an endless stream of sources. But the grading and the quality control and shipping in Third World countries isn't that rigorous. It's getting better, but we started with Cafe Imports, a super reputable importer for specialty coffee. We have a farm in Honduras and two farms in Brazil that we're talking to directly right now. I just got a call from the farmer himself. It's pretty cool to have that accessibility in the 21st century, just to be able to literally talk to the guy in Brazil who's sending you coffee.

It's one of those things. Your sourcing takes time. It takes talking to people, getting referrals. We didn't go into it blind. We asked the guys at Crema in Nashville who they used for sourcing, because they're the ones who trained us how to roast. So for us it was just all referral.

Then it's just finding the bean that you like for the style that you want and just whittling it down and kind of refining it, year after year. It's a long-term approach. If you're going to roast, it's not a quick process. Anyone that thinks it is doesn't know, because it's a true craft. I call it an old-world craft, because there's not any quick way to do it. Coffee's slow. The crops are slow, he shipping's slow. It's a slow industry that requires quick execution. It's quick at the retail end but everything from farm to cup is actually a really slow process that requires *patience and a really good palette and trust*. Old school trust in that what the farmer said he's sending you is what it is, and it's this year's crop and not last year's crop, and it's this grade and not that grade. There's just a whole lot to it. It's been interesting.

Does climate play a role in this? That's a huge variable that's pretty unpredictable.

Oh, for sure. That's the thing. It's sad but there's a lot of risk to the farmer because there's many variables out of their control. Brazil got crushed this past year (2015) because they had a disease run through a lot of their crops. Something like a third of their normal production was cut, which is massive because Brazil's the number one producer of coffee. That kind of fuels the coffee market into a frenzy because of supply and demand.

A lot of people do origin trips. You have to get to know fundamental agriculture. A lot of people, going back to Counterculture and some of those guys, have active people year-round that help the farmers produce the best crops, and institute better growing practices — whether it be technology or knowledge we have in the States — that they might not have access to down there. Sometimes they're not going to have a good crop and a lot of times smaller guys like us don't have multiyear contracts for that very reason, because we can't undertake the risk of having a bad crop arrive and then we're stuck with it. National roasters can do that because they have the control. But there are too many variables out of our control to do multiyear contracts.

But just like the other guys, we'll help mitigate as many of those factors as possible so that we can have consistent crops from the same farmer each year without saying, "Ah, this year we're in, this year we're out." Because then it's just difficult for them. They have bills to pay too and families and communities they're trying to support. We're going to do our best on our end, but it is risky.

You're a "micro-roaster." What does that mean?

That's one of those words. I don't know when you go from micro to macro. I don't know where exactly that cuts off. In my opinion there's definitely a tipping of scales. You'll see some roasters doing mail order, and then all of a sudden, they'll give you the option to grind the coffee before it ships. To me, they're a macro-roaster now because they'll pre-grind coffee. That's just a no-no. Especially coffee, you just don't pre-grind coffee because it ages so quickly. For me that correlates to massive volume, too, because the demand is so high.

A lot of them get outside investment — millions of dollars. Quite a few micro-roasters have scaled up dramatically in the past years, especially on the West Coast where they've had huge investments. When you get that, you have to have returns. So your whole business model changes from small batch to all of a sudden you're doing twenty-pound batches, and then you go to a hundred-and-fifty pound, three hundred pound roasts, which is a big difference. It's just like anything. I don't know if you can maintain the same level of care and specificity on our batches when you start having hundreds of pounds in the roaster, compared to tens. I think that's subjective. There's not a definitive answer.

Tell me about your roasting

We have roasters in each shop. A lot of guys don't do that. They'll have a main place to roast and then they'll ship to their shop. We like that ambience and the tactile experience for customers. We roast about four days a week — a minima of three — just depending on flow and what's going on. You have to roast essentially three days out, so you have to forecast. You can't roast today and brew today. It does require seeing trends and knowing your seasons and so forth.

Coffee is definitely **trial and error**. There are parameters you can find that give you a baseline, then it's figuring out what brew methods you prefer. Then you just taste and taste and taste and tweak and taste. Over time you refine your style through trial and error. In roasting, it's been difficult because I feel like a lot roasters keep their trade secrets to themselves. They don't talk about it that much. I'm not part of the roasters guild yet, so I haven't been to any of their retreats. If you try going online and finding anything about roasting, it'll be all over the map. A lot of it's on home roasting, but there's nothing out there for small commercial roasters like us. It's just trial and error because each bean, each crop, comes in and you just have to find out how that bean works best and how it doesn't work.

I think that's where a really good staff, a trained staff, comes into play. Because an Ethiopian bean might be great through a Bonmac slow pour but might taste really rough through a French press. That's where we stress going through and making sure that we know how each coffee tastes best. We're guiding people with which way they may want it, and which way they won't. Some coffees cool really horribly, so I'll say, "You want to drink this coffee fast because it's delicious hot, but when it gets a little cooler the acid turns on you and it's not that great."

But that's what people aren't used to. We're used to big box retailers, we're used to consistency. A lot of people think the craft is sexy, but with craft, stuff changes weekly. That's the fun part about it. That's the live part about it. That's where you can **keep people on their toes**. But that's also where the struggle is. You find that people almost like homogenization, and they get a little frustrated — "Why can't I just have that same coffee, month after month?" I'm like, "Because it's seasonal and we only have ten bags of it." So that's been a challenge. People like that for a little bit but they want their consistency year-round. But that all comes with us educating them through our day-in and day-out trial and error. There's not a lock-and-load approach. It's just going about it every day and being surprised.

We are different from a lot of the third wave shops. There's kind of a knee-jerk reaction, in my opinion, to Starbucks and those guys where it's, like, no syrups are allowed in third wave shops, and only one size is allowed, and it's a very purist approach.

I'm not like that. We suggest and our proportions are all correct. But we have a regular and a large. We have four syrups on hand. We do mochas. We have seasonal drinks. And that's me kind of conceding to the fact I can still serve great coffee but if they want hazelnut in it, cool. I'm not going to make them feel bad about it. Especially in our environment, it's really cool to watch people start pulling the extras out of their coffee and they're like, "Ah, this is great." Their palette gets refined. You'll see a lot of people do that. They'll switch from whatever their go-to was at Starbucks to just a straight cappuccino here. I don't need to put much cinnamon and whip on it because it's just good as it is. That's where I'm much more subtle in my approach. I think it's necessary to know your market. *If you go in with a self-righteous attitude, I think you may not be around for too long*. You'll alienate a demographic or a large part of the demographic that you really don't necessarily need to. I am a relationship guy. I'm much more about having a community space than I am about maintaining the integrity of the cup of coffee. I just want people to gather. I want to serve great coffee, but I want to be a community spot first and foremost. That's just kind of our ethos.

Tell me about the process of going from one location to two.

It is a big change. We have thirteen employees at our West Palm shop and we have about seventeen in Delray. Different vibe. On the management side it's just difficult because you're just managing people a lot. When you have thirty people that's almost more of a challenge than the logistics of the actual business. Coffee is coffee and I know what the margins should be and what the numbers should be every day. Opening a second one isn't that difficult business-wise, it's just it can be more of my time and energy is spent on the people side, which can detract from focus on other things in the business.

I think two is going to be manageable because my business partner is really amped about this. If we do more than two, we'll definitely have to develop leadership that can take more of that off the plate so I can maintain the feel, the vibe, and the quality of the coffee. That'll be hard. I'm not quite there because we're kind of new in the second one. But, those are the current challenges.

Will you be able to roast at all your locations if you keep growing?

I think we'll always have a roaster, but the roaster can just be smaller and our special bean just for that shop. Or a certain espresso blend that we just roast it at the shop. But I think if we do grow there's going to come a point where we'll centralize all of roasting just for quality control purposes. We have Diedrich IR-12's which are decent sized roasters. I don't think we'll want or need those at other locations if we open them. I'm trying not to look too far in the future about that because if I focus on the growth outside of these first two shops, it just gets me off of making what we have solid. We're a fairly new business.

My partner's been in the restaurant business for thirty years, so he's really established. But he's never done coffee, so it's different than the other ones. We're going to take it a shop at a time.

How do you know when you've found the right location?

Coffee has to be on people's way to wherever they're going. It has to have walk-by traffic. A lot of coffee shops find a really cool spot, and it's just a block or two out of the way, but *that block or two can kill you*. It can mean five hundred people aren't walking past you each day. Your rent might be five hundred bucks less a month, but the impact is dramatically more than that. We're on the main strip in downtown West Palm Beach, and we're on the main strip in Delray. That's essential. It has to be on people's way, and it has to have really easy, available parking.

It can't be a destination. Too many people think their place is going to be the place that everyone will go to, a destination. I think that's a bad move. We're pretty deliberate on having available parking and pretty heavy walk-by traffic, not just drive-by. People tend to just keep on driving. They're just not very focused and they don't really want to pull over. Being in a downtown area, that's why we picked these two, because people are coming here or they're staying here. They're not driving through here. That's what I think is important, at least for what we're doing.

What are some of the things you learned when starting that you hadn't thought of before you got started?

I think a lot of people, me included, underestimate just the liquid cash you should have accessible when you start. You think, "Alright, so I have the build-out paid for" and you tend to spend everything before you open. You think, "Well, we'll make money once we're open." I think that's a bad move. If I had to do it all over again, I'd have more money in the bank just because you're going to have to do a lot of promo. You're going to waste a lot of products. You aren't going to make as much money as you thought you were, because things might happen slower, things break, etc. Usually opening is delayed a lot longer than you thought. There's way more permits that you have to pay for than you had anticipated. There's way more licenses that are a hundred-and-fifty bucks here, a few-hundred-fifty bucks there. A lot of people just focus on paying for the build-out, but they don't really pad their account. I understand because a lot of people don't have access to the capital to cover all that. But I think it's really important. That can make or break it, especially in the first year.

How much capital should you have?

I would say six months is good for us. I would also advise that *if your personal finances are a mess, you probably shouldn't go into business*. A really good litmus test is when I'm talking to people who are considering this, I ask "How are your personal finances?" Not the specifics, but if you have a hard time managing your personal finances, and if you can't figure out ways how to save money then business might not be the place for you. You have to be able to do that. We price out per cup of coffee, lids, cups, coffee, milk, sugar. I know exactly where everything's going. The same thing applies in your personal life. If you don't know where everything's going, then there are going to be a lot of holes in your boat, maybe losing a lot of money. I was always very conscious about accessing my own checking account when I was twelve and had to start buying my own clothes and all that stuff at a very young age. Accounting has always been something that I've had a focus on and been aware of. It's almost natural. But I found that for a lot of people, like my wife, it wasn't like that at all.

We moved in with my brother before we opened the first coffee shop and we just shared rent with him. We had one car instead of two cars. We minimized our lifestyle before we opened the shop. *Don't expect to maintain your same lifestyle*. Minimize it on purpose so that you require the least amount of money when you're starting up. Then, expand it as you can afford to as you grow. I almost put more emphasis on your personal life before you open than I do on your vision of the business, because there's a definite correlation to how you run both and the ability that you'll have to navigate rough waters and make it through and survive.

No matter how diligently you plan, and how conservative you think you are, it will still take longer and cost more, won't it?

Absolutely. For sure. I think that's without a doubt. In my six years of doing this there's never been a time where I'm like, "Oh, that was faster."

It seems like you've taken the long view of your business… "Coffee is slow," "Building relationships with farmers," etc.

I think a lot of people believe they have to grab the lightning. In different industries that may be the case, like the tech world, because it changes so quickly. I think those challenges are completely different.

I had a problem with my partner with this perspective with the Bulletproof Coffee, which is a blend of hot coffee with unsalted butter and MCT oil. My partner said, "Shouldn't we serve Bulletproof Coffee?" I said, "Well, that's a fad." Even during the recession six years ago, the coffee industry didn't dip. We just provide a really good cup down here and do a solid job.

The trends will distract you. You have to have a *clear focus and mission*. Don't chase the wind. For us it's crucial to stick to that, because the temptation's there. You'll think, "Oh, this guy is selling bottled cold brew like crazy." But, nobody'll be talking about it in a year. Or, it'll be such a small impact on your business that it's not worth all the energy and time you're putting into it. Stay the course and know why you're doing what you're doing. And just do it well. Do it in the time that is best, not right now out of a sense of urgency. If you have an urgent approach, you'll set yourself up to make poor decisions.

Kiersten Traina

Liberty Market

GILBERT, AZ

RESTAURANT OWNER SINCE 2008

Tell me how you got started with Liberty Market.

My husband David has cooked as a chef and worked in restaurants the majority of his adult life. He loves food. He's very, very good at cooking things and it comes very naturally to him. My background is very different in that I have degrees in education and special ed. I went to college at Nebraska and really thought I was going to teach. David and I met one night when he was cooking a dinner and I was serving the dinner. We were both a little bit older and I actually took his chef's knives and cut a whole box of mushrooms on a granite countertop without a cutting board. The fact that we're even together is a miracle because no chef would ever allow that to happen.

We met and I realized that I like teaching and I like education, but I really, really love my husband and I love what he does. My skill set matched his very well. And so we started catering together. We had a lot of friends that were getting married so we decided to start a catering company. We ended up catering our own wedding, which I don't recommend to anyone on the planet.

We go to church in Gilbert and after church we'd drive past this building that was a grocery store called Liberty Market. We would drive by it and just say, "Whoever gets that building better not screw it up." Then we got on the freeway and we'd go to lunch and go home. We did that for about two years. And then out of the blue, a friend of ours who is also a really good restaurateur in Gilbert, called us. We had just gotten back from China and were dealing with jet lag. I was in the house, Dave was outside on the phone, and he comes back in and he goes, "Kiersten, that was Joe Johnston*. He wants to know if we want to open a restaurant with him at Liberty Market. Do you know where you put my toothpaste?" And I'm going, "Do I know where I put your tooth…wait a second…What about a restaurant?" That was in about 2005. We sat down with Joe and we sought a lot of guidance and asked people, "Should we do this? We know that the restaurant business is really, really hard. Is this something that we should look at doing?" Every person that we talked said yes. Some of the best advice we got was, "If you hadn't told us it was Joe Johnston, we would tell you go find Joe Johnston and do it with him."

We had loved this building for years. We were good friends with Joe. My husband Dave always says that business partnerships are a lot like a marriage. We felt really comfortable with Joe and his wife Cindy opening

*Joe was featured in the first Restaurant Owners Uncorked book

this. We started planning it in 2005. It took us three years to plan it, which is a long time. Most people don't take three years to plan a restaurant, they want to get open as soon as they can. But it was very, very good for us in that we were able to process through all of the questions that we could anticipate, so that when we opened the questions that we couldn't anticipate where the ones that we had to focus on. I think that made it a little bit easier. We did open though, on the second worst day of the stock market, in October of 2008. We opened at pretty much the ***worst possible time that anyone could open a restaurant***. But we just celebrated eight years in business and for us it is a huge tribute to God's grace that we are even serving people, considering how many restaurants didn't make it through that period of time.

Three years is a long time to plan!

I don't know how most people would do it, but if anyone were to ask me I would tell them to do it how we did. The building is from the 1930's, so there was a lot of construction that had to go into it. We had to put in what's called a "moment frame," which is a frame in case there were to be an earthquake. There was a ton of construction that had to be done.

Then we also had to figure out the serving style. Did we want to be fast casual? Fast casual wasn't very popular. I don't even think people really knew you could do that. So we kind of created a serving system that works for us. You come in, you stand in line. You walk past our pizza station, you walk past our salad station, you walk past the desserts. You place your order. And then from that point in time, we do everything full service. We bring your food out, we refill cups if you need them, that sort of thing. It's kind of a hybrid that we created to work our system. Our seating is unique in that when you're in line we have a hostess that goes down the line, gives you a number and puts a number on a table so you never have to wonder where you're going to sit. We find that for you. We were coming up with those things and how those work.

We had to build a kitchen. Dave had worked in kitchens that you could go in in the morning when it was dark, there could be a hurricane, and when you came out, it was dark. You had no idea that even happened. So, we put in tons of natural light. Our kitchen is glassed in so you can watch people cook. Our dish room has a huge window so there's natural light in that as well. We just wanted to honor the people that work for us as much as the people that come in because that's as important as anything else.

I did all the paperwork. My degrees and my writing in college really helped. We wrote **vignettes** on the type of people that we thought would come in. We really felt like there would be families that came in. We wrote what we wanted their experience to be like. We thought there would be people that came in for business meetings so we wrote what their experience would be like. Moms who dropped their kids off for school — I think there were five different vignettes that we wrote. Then we took all of those vignettes and asked, "If it's moms with kids, what do we feed kids? If it's business people, how do we make lunch gets done in an hour? If it's families that come in for a holiday, how do we make sure we have seating that will fit a family of six, seven, eight or nine?" All of those pieces were thought through.

With the menu, we didn't want it to be one kind of food. Dave is Sicilian so we wanted a little bit of Italian in there, but not so heavy that it was an Italian restaurant. What do those pieces look like? How does this work? We wrote out all of those things. To this day, if I were to say I don't know if I want to open a second restaurant, it would only be because of that second piece of this puzzle. I took every single menu item, with Dave's help, and we wrote out the process for it, from how it was cooked, what walk-in did you go in, what shelf did you get it off, what pan did you put it in, what plate did you put it on, where did you take it? We walked through those steps so that you could literally follow a process to get food. Then we did that with customers as well. When you come up, what do you order? Where does your food go? Where do you sit? Where do you get your drinks? We wrote out literally every piece of a day at Liberty Market with every menu item. It was exhausting for me. I was like, "Why am I doing this? This is ridiculous." It was so hard to do, until the day that I did the sandwiches. I'm writing out the sandwiches, and I realize we have put all of our reach-ins on the wrong side, so that the doors don't open correctly. The sandwich guy had to walk around an aisle to get the stuff out and come back around. Had we not done that preparation, we would have had to change it after we opened. After that, even though it was time-consuming, it helped us to really get a better picture of what we were going to be asking our employees to do. It enabled us just to really see it *from the eyes of our employees*. And then things like if you come in this way, is this an easy line to get in? Or do you have walk through things? Or do we have to move this here? The three years really enabled us to be a little bit wiser from the perspective of the people that would be in the restaurant that weren't the owners.

I would imagine that requires an extreme amount of patience.

What it really did for Dave and I is that it helped me understand the kitchen, and it helped him understand the front of the house a little bit from what my perspective would be. I ran front of the house and I could be telling him, "Hey, this is going to be wrong." I would know it because that's where I was going spend all of my time and I would have thought about that. He would say, "Well, no, this is kitchen. You have to look at this." It helped us kind of solidify as a married couple, but also as a married couple who's going to spend an inordinate amount of time together in a very stressful situation. I served all through college and we both remember too clearly that the front of the house and the back of house in all of the restaurants we worked at didn't like each other. If there is something wrong, front of the house would always say, "It's your fault" and back of the house would say, "No, it's your fault." We realized pretty quickly we had to *bridge that gap*. If we didn't figure out how to bridge that gap personally, it was going to affect our marriage. It really caused us to try and understand where each of us were coming from, from a different perspective. This helped the staff, which helped our customers, which helped us as a married couple. I think Joe and Cindy would say the same thing. Going through all of these pieces really helped bind us together as an ownership team, too, because all of us knew what was going on in the restaurant. It wasn't like, "Well, Kiersten's only doing this, David's only doing this, Joe's only doing this and Cindy's doing that." Yes, we were doing our job, but each of us then knew what the responsibilities of the other person, or the other individuals were. That really helped us. Much like we talked about a partnership being a marriage, it really helped us as married couples and as business partners to be more effective.

Do you still go back and revisit this process?

We do a lot. We've been able to really grow a staff that I love. I don't know how many business owners can say that and see their staff beyond employees. I really feel like our staff is an *extension of our family*. We argue and we disagree and we do all the things family do. But there's a loyalty and a common goal. I think that's huge. One of the things that we talked a lot about, and we come back to this all of the time, is we only train our staff on two things besides how to do what you do – one is a passion for the food and the second one is serving with a servant's heart. We evaluate that regularly. If you make a pizza and the pizza is burned on the bottom and maybe the busser is helping carry something out because they have a free minute and they see that the pizza's burnt, the passion for the food is that even though it's a busser who might not have a lot to do with the making of the pizza, they can stop that process and say, "Hey, I don't think we can serve that." We encourage them to do that. We'll remake it because it's everyone's responsibility to have a passion for the food.

And then serving with a servant's heart is that you serve out of an internal desire to serve people, not because they tip and not because you get a paycheck. There's a difference when you go into a business where people are serving because they care versus serving because you're paying their rent. Both accomplish the same thing. They get a paycheck. They make tips. They pay rent. But one is done with a different heart motivation, and that's really proven to be an amazing thing that we see in our staff.

We go back and evaluate things, we go back and say, "Okay, let's look at the things we're doing." We just did an update on our menu. And it's like, "Okay, let's look at all these pieces on the menu." We have to have a passion for the food, so that whether Dave's making the eggplant parmesan, or Chris is, or Jordan is, or Jade is, it all looks the same because we all have the same passion for the food.

And then looking at how we do things, we have to decide, What are we changing? How do we reevaluate this? Do we need to change? Are we doing sticky buns on the weekend? Or do we do them during the week? How is that caring for our customers? How is that serving from the heart? If it's something people want, can we do that and serve them in that way? We do evaluate constantly, asking ourselves is this what we want, and is this what we see. Owners' eyes are different sometimes. You go in you see all of the things that you need to fix. In that framework of serving with a servant's heart and having a passion for the food, it enables us to go back and ask those questions and change those things based on our core tenets to make the restaurant better for other people and the employees that work with us.

How do you get your staff to share that same mentality and serve from the heart with a passion for the food?

We've been really, really blessed with our staff. Gilbert has a very young population. We have a lot of teenagers that start with us. We have older people too, but it's really fun to watch these teenagers come in. It's their first job and empowering them to say if you don't like this or if you think something's wrong, you have to let us know because this is part of your job, too. We take them through that training and teach them those tenets. We take them through Liberty Market 101. Here's how we started, this is what this looks like, here's what our hearts are. *This is your place.* We don't just hire you to check you off and say, "Okay, we have someone bussing dishes." We want you to be a part of this. Our leadership staff that we've had — and we've had a couple people that have been with us the full time — they have taken this on themselves. We had a difficult situation a couple of years ago with a new hire. Several of our employees came to us to talk about it. They didn't say, "We don't like this person. We don't want this to happen. We don't want this, etc." They came and they said, "This person is adjusting the culture that we believe in, and we can't work here if that culture isn't here anymore — that culture of caring for others and passion for the food." That was more meaningful than anything that we would have seen, because our staff said that the culture that we want to work in is being upset, and we need to get that back. We need to make sure that is what we do, because that's what Liberty Market is. We've been able to train that into some people, and we just have people that have heart and values that have stepped up to that plate and it's fascinating to watch them train this staff, and say, "This is what *we* do." It's not what Dave and Kiersten, Joe and Cindy want, it's what *we* do at Liberty Market.

We hired a guy named Andy a couple years ago. He came to us and said, "I'm really interested in consulting with restaurants. Is there any way that we could trade? I'll consult with you and we'll go through some things and I'll trade off that and we'll be able to use your name as having experience with this." It has been one of the most valuable experiences ever. What he's really good at is teaching a staff to ask questions. So instead of saying, "You need to fill up those salt shakers," I'll say, "Hey, when you get to a table and this is where you're sitting down and you need salt, what is one of the things you look at?" It's exactly the same thing – you've got to fill the salt shaker up. But he has trained and worked with our staff and with Dave and just developed this culture of education and this culture of learning. Instead of being top-down-do-this-because-I-said-it, they **lead from example**, and they **lead from asking questions**. We call them a leadership team, not a manager leader team, because they are not managing people and they are leading people by example. We've really tried to put words in that and create the vocabulary of what we want to do. We call them "service professionals" instead of wait staff, "kitchen professionals" instead of cooks, because it means a little bit more. It explains more when you read those words and you see those words. When I'm a professional, I'd better act like a professional. By putting those words in and creating our own take on that, we accomplish the same thing but in a way that gives value to people that we see value in.

How do you keep people engaged and a part of your team with so much devotion when you have a single location and that's the place that they're going to be as long as they're with you?

What I had to realize very quickly is that there are different kinds of restaurateurs. You have restaurateurs whose goal is to open five or open ten, and that's just a natural progression. You have one, it's running well, we're going to open a second one. It's running well, and now have a system we're going to follow. But we adopted a little girl about four-and-a-half years ago. We really like the fact that Dave's home on a regular basis. We really like the fact that I can take her to school and pick her up and we can go on vacation because we have a staff that stays there. We have personally realized that we are the kind of owners where one Liberty Market concept is where we're at. We can pour our time and attention into what we do, and there are always things that we see that we can do better and things that we can create. Dave is there on a regular basis. We had a situation a couple weeks ago, where one of our cooks was out so our sous chef just stepped up and picked up his shifts. When she was on day seven of just picking up this person's shift along with her own, Dave called and said, "Hey, it's my day off. I'm coming in, I'm going to work your shift. You just take the day off." So, he went in on one of his days off. He had the ability to do that because we have a single location. Our staff sees that we value them. He could have taken his day off, but that's what we do. You have a lot of restaurateurs that have a different perception of being in the restaurant. It doesn't work for us. When he covered that shift she said, "You have no idea how much that meant to me." It was probably just six hours out of Dave's life — it was no big deal. But that created this, "Wow, you care for me. You were aware that I worked seven days straight. You were aware that I did this for the restaurant, and you value that."

If you've worked enough places, you begin to see that something's different. We close Christmas Eve and Christmas Day every year. That was a little selfish because Christmas Eve is my favorite day of the year. I was like, "I'm not opening a restaurant where I can't take my days off. So we're going to close Christmas Eve and Christmas Day. And if we're not going to close Christmas Eve and Christmas Day, we're not going to open ever." I don't have to work seven days a week anymore, so it's really easy for me to schedule myself Christmas Eve and Christmas Day off and never even think about it. That doesn't affect me. But we still close Christmas Eve and Christmas Day, even though Christmas Eve's an incredibly good business day for us, because it gives our staff two days at home with their families for the holidays. It's all of those things where you get that gratitude and they'll say, "Wow, we really appreciate that." I'll read their social media sometimes and they'll say, "I love having a boss who lets me have two days off." It's a pretty big hit financially, but what we feel from the benefit of giving them Christmas off is more valuable to us than the money we would make. We work to give them good wages and we try to communicate with them. I really hope what they see is that *it's not about filling our pockets with money*, it's about a place that's home for us, and they're part of that home.

You spent all that time planning down to very important details. Were there any things you had not thought of?

We opened our first day and I was so excited at about five o'clock in the morning and I left at midnight, got home, crawled in bed, and just sobbed. Dave goes, "What's wrong?" And I'm like, "We have to do this again tomorrow! And then the day after that. And then the day after that." I hadn't been aware of how exhausting it would be, or how taxing it would be. I didn't know that we would have to fight to stay open all the time. It was a recession – people might not come to your restaurant. One of the things that Dave and I were talking about right after we opened was how to cut costs. How do we make sure we stay open? What do we change? He said, "Kiersten, I had no idea I would feel so responsible for employees. We may not make it. We might end up closing and you and I would figure out what to do with that and we would move on and we would go from there. But I didn't think of if we close, how that affects fifty employees. I cannot directly handle the weight of that stress." I remember going, "If we didn't care for employees, this would be a whole lot easier." We could be like, "I don't really care if you don't want to be open on Christmas Eve – we're opening." But that weight of caring for another person and another person's family — I didn't realize how deeply that would affect us, and how important that would become to us.

One of the crazy things we did was open with a very Italian breakfast. We did paninis. We have a forty-five hundred square foot restaurant. We have over a hundred seats inside, and probably another thirty-five or forty outside, so we're a pretty big establishment. We did a breakfast that was maybe two panini sandwiches, maybe yogurt and granola — that does not add up to staying open if you do the math. Within about three weeks, Dave and Joe had to sit down and put together an entire breakfast menu that we had not vetted like we did everything else. We went from a really commuter breakfast to a full breakfast within three weeks. You have to have that mentality of nothing's sacred. Dave didn't really ever want to make pancakes – it wasn't his favorite thing to do. We talked and realized if we don't have pancakes, you'll never get a kid in this restaurant. We put pancakes on the menu. Now we have four different kinds of pancakes, and we do them well. That ability to not hold anything sacred enables you to be flexible enough to stay in business. I think you have to stay sacred with the things that are foundational, like serving with a servant's heart and having a passion for the food. But if you want to have that salad because your grandma always made that salad that way and so help you, you have to put that stuff in it — but nobody's eating it — it's prideful if you're not willing to take it off. ***Pride will kill you*** in this business.

Even with breakfast, when you look at that and go, "Okay, we have a passion for good food. We're making the best Paninis we could possibly make. But if we don't change that, we're not doing a very good job of serving with a servant's heart because we're not serving people who can't come in." We said this was a great idea and would be great if we lived somewhere in Italy where there were forty-seven million tourists every year and they wanted Italian food this way. I live in a community that is the second highest population of per capital income in the state of Arizona, and everybody out here has children. How do I serve those people what they'd like and how do I make that analogous to what we do and how we do that? We have an espresso bar. When we opened it, it was that big thing where you could never have syrups — the coffee's bad if you put syrup in it. Well, if we didn't put vanilla or offer vanilla latte, our espresso bar wouldn't be frequented as much because a very big draw are flavored lattes and that sort of thing. Our integrity was that we want a passion for the food, so we had to balance those things together. What we decided to do is make our own syrups from scratch. We use really good ingredients — it's very simple to make vanilla flavoring. We said, "We want to serve people what they want, which was a vanilla latte, and we want to serve it with the integrity that we feel food should have. One way we're going to do that is by making our own syrups and making everybody happy." It's very cost effective to make your own syrups. We don't have forty-seven thousand syrups – I think we have four. Our caramel is made from scratch, our chocolate is made from scratch, and our four syrups are made from scratch. We were able to stay relevant to what we feel is important but serve and care for people which we also feel is important. We try to take what is foundational, but then also be flexible, and meld those together.

When you see those smiling, happy children and their happy parents who are glad you have pancakes, even if it wasn't what you initially wanted, does it help you turn on some passion for that?

It does. And everybody thinks we have the best pancakes. You look at that and say, "Hey, if we're going to make pancakes let's make the best pancakes we can." We didn't have a kid when we started doing pancakes. If we didn't have pancakes, four-and-a-half years ago we would have added pancakes because I'm taking my kid into the restaurant and I want her to have pancakes. I think you have to say, "What stage of life am I in? I need to glimpse around and look at other people. I need to get outside of myself and see what that looks like. If I had a kid, what does this look like? If I had an elderly parent coming in, how do I have seating for them so they can wait instead of standing in line?" In serving with a servant's heart, you begin to have to look outside of yourself and look at other people. We live in a society where we look at ourselves first and then we'll look at other people if it benefits us. We have a responsibility to train our staff to be better people in general anyway, so in addition to teaching them about good food I teach them other skills much like I would my daughter. By teaching them to look at other people and to care for other people, that doesn't necessarily make the world a completely better place, because they might not think of other people outside of the restaurant, but it does make this slice of the world a little better because we are thinking about other people. And as an educator and as a person who has faith, I feel like that is something that we can offer. People might not know why it's different, but it's very different.

Do you think years ahead about the future of Liberty Market? Or do you just think about taking it one day at a time?

I think that guides Dave's and my life in general, from raising kids to having a home, to having a business. It's the unique principle of two hands. You have one hand that you have closed and hold tightly to the right now, and you have one hand that's open for the not yet. *You have to live in the tension of looking at both of those things*. Looking at the restaurant business leaves me terrified. I read an article the other day on the restaurant bubble breaking. You could look at that and go, "Oh my gosh, I've got to do all these things. We have to change this. And we have to do this and that." You have to look at staying relevant without changing your message. Arizona just went through a significant law change that changed our minimum wage requirements which in turn affected ninety-five percent of what we pay our staff. We have to look at that and say, "Okay, how do we adjust menu prices? How do we adjust all of these things to be able to make up for the wage difference?" But then, how do we also look at that and go, "How do we stay in business in five years?" You have to adjust your prices, but instead of doing a blanket change across the board and raising all of our prices this way, it was very strategic. We looked at it and said, "We can raise this price but keep this price the same." This enables us to pay our employees more right now, but looking at the future ensures that we're not working ourselves out of a restaurant or pricing ourselves out of a restaurant. It's this tension that we're constantly in – how do we continue to move forward, but continue to do what we're doing.

You could have a conversation with yourself on the day before you opened your doors, knowing what you know now, what would you say?

I would want to tell her, "You're not going to die. You're going to make it. And it will be better that you could ever think it will be." I think there were times when I was so in the moment that I thought, "I don't know how to do this. I can't do this." Yet I feel like that for every one of those situations, as a person of faith, I feel like God gave me what I needed. He didn't give me more than I needed. He gave me what I needed to get through that day and just push through it and establishing processes and things that would work, day to day. "Kiersten, you're going to make it." It's going to be a great lesson to look back and see faithfulness. I think that's what I would say.

What I would also encourage for people is to tell their story. ***When you tell your story, it becomes so real***. You see, "Wow, it was really tough. But look at what happened here." I appreciate you giving me the opportunity to sit down and just relive eight-and-a-half years of what we have done, to see where we started and to know where that story began, and to see where it is now. And then to be excited about where it's going as well.

Keith Santangelo

Bourbon Street Bar & Grille

NEW YORK, NY

RESTAURANT OWNER SINCE 2014

You started as the GM and now you're now the owner. Tell me about that journey.

It was a really cool opportunity and interesting journey. I started here as the general manager in the very beginning of 2009. I was here until 2013 and then I went to help out at one of other bars. I took over a turnaround project, and in the process of being there got a phone call from the partners here. I got invited back to buy a couple of them out and become the owner after being the GM and director of operations here for a long time. That was the *phone call of a lifetime* for me. I've just been in love with the place for a long time. I was born and raised in South Louisiana, so it was a fit for me and I fell in love with the place. I'm just delighted that it's mine and my partner's now. We're having a blast.

Had you always wanted to own a restaurant or was it just something about this specific opportunity?

I think I've always wanted to. It sounds like a cliché, but it's really true – it kind of chose me. I didn't have a choice. I grew up in a family that was half Italian and half Cajun French. I grew up with my dad owning his own butcher shops and grocery stores and delis and stuff. I grew up around food. I'm a little biased, but I don't think there's any better life introduction to the hospitality business then just growing up that way. Every single thing we did involved a lot of people, a lot of family, and delicious food and drinks, whether it was the Italian side or the Cajun side. I was very lucky with my exposure to culinary things and family get-togethers at a very young age. So, I think it kind of chose me.

Was your partner already a part of the business?

He was actually here a little bit before me in 2008 as one of the nighttime bartenders. He became the bar manager over the course of the time that I was the general manager. We were both here for a long time. We became friends. We were great friends with the previous owners as well. We both went to take over that other project that I was talking about. It was within the family — one of their other bars. They have many businesses, and it was one of the other ones we went to turnaround. In the meantime, they called us both back up while we were there and asked us if we were interested in coming back together. We certainly were. We were hoping for that. I don't know if we knew it would work out exactly this way, but, for both of us it was a long-term goal to eventually open our own place. So, it worked out perfectly.

What advice would you give on finding the right partner?

I don't have the key. But I would say that if you haven't worked with him or her for a few years, I don't think you really know. I would suggest that you know them very intimately. We talk a lot between colleagues and other peers. We say all the time that having a partner is just like being married. It really is. You're attached. You have a baby together. Unless the worst happens, you're not going your separate ways. You really better be able to work together and trust each other and work out problems together when they come up. Because, you have a common baby. *I've seen a lot of business fall apart based on partnerships.* I think it's imperative that you know anyone that you decide to go into business with, that you know them and you know them well and you know how they work and that it's a good fit. I think it's worth taking the time to figure that out before having a business fail and then figuring out how to chop it up between the two or three or four of you. That's something no one wants to do. It's worth the time to get to know people and make sure your partners are the right fit for you.

How did you finance going from a GM to an owner?

That's a challenge. In my case, it was a combination of all things. If you're saving and you're planning on it, you're hoping for an opportunity. The second part of it is you're going around trying to get a loan. Especially in the last five years, that's been a tough aspect of it — getting someone to believe in you, a bank to finance you or partner with you as you buy in. I was lucky in that I was buying into a business that had a proven track record of success and had been open for a while. I think that certainly helped. I can't imagine going to sit down in front of somebody and asking for money for just me and my original idea, and I had nothing else behind that. That's got to make it even more difficult and the people that figure that out, I just really admire.

I've heard a ton of great stories being in this industry. And I've been doing this since I was sixteen. I moved to New York from Louisiana when I was eighteen, and I started serving, waiting tables and bartending. I've been doing this for a long time. It's an industry that I've paid close attention to since I was very young. I've heard some great stories about people bootstrapping and working three jobs and putting some savings away to get things started. And I've heard other stories like mine where you get an opportunity and you have a little savings and you're able to finance the rest of it. I think there's more than one way to skin that cat. None of them are very easy. But, they are doable and it is very worth it. It's a unique breed of people. But if you're a restaurant owner and you know that, there's nothing else you'd rather be doing. So, it is worth it.

How have you tried to instill that sense of ownership in your team?

Certainly I hope for that. I look for it. Sometimes it's a trait that people just possess. Sometimes that level of caring isn't always something you can train. I think it's very important in the hiring process to try and identify the right candidates. Some of it is untrainable. Some of it is personality. Some of it is natural, genuine hospitality.

There's something that has always stuck with me from Danny Meyer's book, *Setting the Table*. It's just absolute required reading for anyone who wants to manage or own in this business. He always talked about hiring fifty-one percent on hospitality and forty-nine percent on technical skill. And I've tried to carry that with me. It really resonated with me. In the hiring process, I look for people who have that natural ability, who genuinely want to be hospitable, and maybe naturally treat things like it's their own and naturally take that ownership mentality. I do try and instill it in my people. I sell it to them because it serves them as well as it serves us. *I'm always hoping that managers that I hire will open their own place someday*. That's the natural progression of things. I hope it helps them learn for their future endeavors. And in the meantime, it serves our operation very well.

What are some of the guiding principles that you use at Bourbon Street?

It sounds so cheesy and corny and people might not buy it, but it's really, really true – I just push the hospitality aspect of it all the time. I want everyone that works here to *genuinely care about the guests*. Being in New York City and being a Louisiana-themed restaurant, I always say that it's our hospitality that should set us apart. Competing on food in New York City — you've got the likes of Per Se and Eleven Madison Park and Grammercy Tavern. Do we want to try and set ourselves apart from some of the greatest culinary restaurants in the world? We certainly want to give great food, great value. Everything here is scratch and it's a unique menu, and it's a unique experience. But again, you're dealing with Per Se and Le Bernardin and all those places. And then the other thing is price. We don't really want to compete on price. We don't want to be the cheapest guys on the block. The way that we can set ourselves apart is with the ambience and the hospitality. When people walk in here they really do feel welcome. They feel like they're being welcomed home. And they get genuine hospitality. Whatever it takes, we go above and beyond to make the guest feel special. That's how we try to set ourselves apart. To deliver that you have to hire right, and that is the hardest part of the process. That's a principle that we try to live and die by. You have to hire the right people and luckily, we have a great staff. The staff selection has always been good. If you can find the right people to buy into what you're doing and genuinely deliver that hospitality, I think it's been something that's set us apart.

What is unique about operating a restaurant in New York?

The benefit is the volume — the density of people that are here walking up and down the street. It's New York City. There's always something happening. People are in and out every day. So, the benefit is the volume and what's going on and your proximity to guests. The density of the population in the tiny island is what sustains this number of restaurants.

The flip side of that, though, is there is an incredible amount of competition. Places are opening and closing all the time. Even *being here six years feels like a victory*. Thank goodness we're doing great and I hope we're here for thirty more. But there is a lot of competition. The rents are a challenge. In 2012 we got a great advocacy group, the New York City Hospitality Alliance, which is a great alliance for the hospitality industry. That has been a big help. One of the biggest challenges in New York City is the regulatory environment. The City itself has imposed a lot of things on the restaurant industry as of late, like paid sick leave and raising the minimum wage each year.

There's also the Health Department inspections with the letter grades. We've always had an "A." We love hanging an "A" in the window because we love for the guests to feel confident when they come in here. But the fines that come along with that are a challenge at times. No one wanted the letter grades at first, but if you're hanging an "A" and you're doing your job, an "A" really is achievable. It's a challenge, but it's achievable. And if you're hanging an "A" and everyone else on your block isn't, it gives you an opportunity to thrive.

There are a lot of inspections and a lot of city agencies and things like that. The compliance is more difficult than it might be other places. And the rent is, of course, high. If you navigate it properly and you operate well, you really can do well. But, the competition is very, very high. With so much turnover, the longer you're there people just have more confidence. People feel more familiar with the brand and you become homey to them. You become like a go-to.

What keeps your fire burning as a restaurant owner and makes you want to get up every day and do it again and again?

The thing that keeps the fire going is that, and it sounds cliché, you genuinely love what you do. I love having people here, and groups here. I love walking around the floor and seeing people that I know that have been here many times. I love having them celebrate their anniversaries here, their birthday parties here, bridal showers, wedding showers. We just had a baby shower. And especially when it's people that you start to know, it's part of your community. That gives me genuine joy. I love providing an environment where people can come and celebrate their life occasions and have good food and great drinks. I love being a part of the community. I think that goes back to those roots I was talking about in the very beginning. My entire life growing up involved family and friends coming together over food and drinks and just celebrating life. Whatever the occasions were, that's how it always happened around me and my family. I get genuine joy out of that and doing that for other people.

I also just *love the business*. We haven't gone too far talking about opening up the next place or not, but I have tons of ideas and I really love that aspect of it. I love all of the different cuisines and different concepts. We enjoy the creative part of it. What could we come up with next? What sort of place can we open? All the different things that go into that is a secondary love.

What is a typical day like?

It starts pretty early. I'm almost always up by six a.m. I feel better when I start my day early. I'm a family guy — I have a wife and three kids. I usually get up early with my kids and start them off and get them to school. Then I head into work. I'm usually here about nine a.m. and that's a quiet hour. Usually the staff's in around ten. We're open every day from eleven a.m. to four a.m. That quiet first hour is probably the most important hour in my day, because I get in my calendar. I get in my task list. I figure out exactly what today needs to hold, and prioritize and we get started. I'm here from nine a.m. usually until around seven or eight p.m., unless there's something going on later at night that I want to be here for. Sometimes we have big events or special occasions and things like that I stick around for. But I have a couple nighttime managers that come in at that point. I usually stay through the dinner service. It's a bar as well, so we're open until four a.m. I'll let the PM Manager sort of bring it home for the day. I spend a lot of time in the office and I try and spend as much time as I can with my management team and on the floor with my staff and seeing the guests. It is a lot of hours — fifty, sixty, sometimes more hours per week is not unheard of, especially depending on what you have going on. But, you get a reward out of it. ***It's worth it***. And you're used to it. Thank God I met my wife in the same industry. I have a wife who understands. I wouldn't know what to say to someone who hadn't also been in the industry. My wife was a restaurant manager when I met her. Luckily, she understands most times when I say I'll be home at five and actually come home at eleven p.m. or midnight, so I'm very lucky.

Do you worry about finding balance if you expand and open another location?

I honestly think that is probably one of the hardest things to do. I was listening to an interview with Danny Meyer, author of *Setting the Table*, and he was saying the hardest thing he ever did was go from one to two. And then from two to three. And then after three, there was sort of a system in place, an infrastructure in place to continue to grow. I think three and beyond is somewhat easier than one to two or two to three. I think that's the hardest part because you don't have a head office or an infrastructure in place to keep growing. It's you. How do you take your eye off of this to go do the second thing, and replace yourself? When you're an owner of one place you're doing a fulltime job. If you're going to go spend any time working on the second concept or the second place, someone has to pick up where you left off. I think it's a really difficult transition.

I'm lucky that I have two managers that have worked with me, side by side, for four or five years. I don't know if there's any replacing that. Having someone work with you and next to you for four or five years, I have a great level of confidence that they understand exactly what we're trying to achieve and that they share the same passion. I would feel confident using some of our long-term staff members to help us grow. But I would definitely need that help. If I didn't have that, I really don't know. I think it would a much more difficult proposition, a much more difficult undertaking, to try and keep your eye on a bunch of places at once when you don't have people who share exactly what your vision and your goal is and exactly how you're trying to achieve it. I think that would be really hard. I think once you have things in place, it's a little bit easier to keep growing. When you're going from one to two, it's like redoing everything for the first time. It's a challenge I hope to take.

If you could have a conversation with yourself before you purchased the business — would you do it again? Would you do anything differently?

I would definitely do it again. It's been a genuine joy for me, and I mean that. You read a lot of advice books about this industry, and a lot of times they start out and they say if you could do anything else, do that. But if you can't, if all you can do to be happy is work in a restaurant, then this industry might be for you. And you might have success. It's true — it's a tough industry. But I genuinely can't see myself doing anything else. I really love it. So, I would definitely do it again. I wouldn't tell myself to do anything different. I think what I would tell myself is that there are going to be ups and down, and you have to be prepared for that. I was so stressed out a lot of times. There was the one week that we'd be down, and then of course, the next three weeks we'd break records for sales. But, you're living and dying by the sales and your performance as an owner, and it's yours, not just the mentality but really it's yours, you have a tendency to stress yourself out and want everything to be perfect. I would definitely do it again but the advice I would give is there's going to be ups and downs, there's going to be busy weeks, there's going to be slow weeks. Everything's not going to go perfect all the time, but it's going to be okay. It's still going to be successful. And it has been. But I would tell my younger self to *relax a little bit*. I would tell him not to stress out over every detail so much. If you trust in your philosophy and your people and you hire the right people, it's going to go the right way. I would definitely try to micro-manage less if I could go back, and try and stress out less over every single detail as you do in the beginning. Some of it's just the nature of the beast – you're going to do it. You're going to check every menu and you're going to check every reservation and maybe that was a contributor to the success. But in hindsight, something you learn after you're the boss for a while is that you really do yourself a service by hiring the right people, empowering and trusting them and building a team around you. When you do that, everything gets easier. Everything, all your success, comes a little easier.

What are some of the things that concern you about the business?

Some things do keep me awake at night. One thing just kept me awake at night this week was we had to raise our prices pretty heavily. Price rises keep me awake at night. But they're a hundred percent necessary. The labor force and the price rises keep me awake at night. There's a lot of uncertainty in the industry right now. It gets more complicated. In New York City, you have clients all over the U.S. and maybe even beyond that. You're dealing with a lot of different things. But New York City recently put in this fifteen-dollar minimum wage. We're climbing towards that. Servers that used to make five dollars an hour are soon going to make much, much more. They've been given raises each of the beginning of the last two years and that's going to continue for the next two or three years until we reach that plateau. Same for dishwashers that used to make eight dollars an hour and now make thirteen and then they're going to make fifteen. I think the minimum wage rise is great for the workforce. Something that is more of a living wage for them is the right way to go. We want to take care of our people. But what comes along with that is paying for it. Restaurants in New York City are going to raise their prices every single year in order to pay for the rise in eighty percent of their workforce. That keeps me up at night because that's a lot of uncertainty. What's going to happen with that? When prices go up forty percent over the next two or three years, you have to wonder how the public is going to react to that. But, it's going to happen across the board because otherwise people are going to go out of business. The margins in this industry, as most people know, are already pretty thin. There's no way for the industry to sustain those kind of labor wage hikes without rising prices. Right now, that keeps me up, pretty regularly. It's a *very uncertain time* for that. And I don't like raising prices. Most people probably don't believe that. Everyone likes to make money. But, I'm sure other restaurateurs understand – you don't like raising prices and hitting your guest with a new price every time they come in. We want to make money but we also want to take care of our guests. We want to offer a great value. You're always toeing that line – you're always trying to balance that.

What are some of the behind-the-scenes aspects of the business that could be difference makers in whether a restaurant succeeds or not?

On a perfect day, it could look like a really great job. Overall, I still think it is and I love it. On a perfect day for someone outside looking in, it can look like a lot of fun. You're like, "Oh, you just meet with reps and you have a few glasses of wine and you oversee people serving dinner and watch a football game on the bar screen and this seems great. I could do this." But the reality is, to make it a success there's a lot of hours that people don't see behind the scenes. In my case, I'm someone who always *closely watches the financials*. I've always excelled at the office aspect of the job. There's a lot of hours that go into managing your inventories and managing your finances and keeping a close eye on all of your margins and your operating costs and your profitability, your prime costs — things like that. I think it's imperative to manage those things properly and isolate mistakes really quickly when you have them happen. It's also a lot of hours spent being in touch with your staff and developing relationships. All those things happen behind the scenes. If you're an owner of a small operation, there are a lot of office hours that go into it that most people do not see. But if you're going to manage your books properly and you're going to manage your finances properly and really be on the pulse of your business, there's a lot of hours behind the scenes that people don't know about.

What are some of the things that people may not think about before they get involved in starting or buying a restaurant?

I think there could be a lot of things. I've gone to a lot of meetings with prospective restaurant owners. One of the first things that usually happens, whether it be a workshop or a class or whatever it is, they'll say, "Raise your hand if you've ever worked in a restaurant." I'm always shocked at the amount of hands that don't go up. I'm always shocked at the amount of people that have never worked in a restaurant that aspire or try to open their own restaurant. When I go to these classes and I talk to a lot of these perspective owners, the first thing they need to do is go work in a restaurant. I think there's a lot of things they might not know. I think people make a lot of assumptions about what owning a restaurant or a bar might be like. And I think it could be very different than what they think.

What a lot of people don't realize is that you wear a lot of hats. It's not all glamorous. A lot of times you're in a basement plunging things and not sipping wine and talking to clients and having fun. It does give me great joy. It is a great job if it's what you want to do. But, I think people underestimate the amount of hats you have to wear if you own a restaurant and just how difficult it can be. Everyone is familiar — I *think* — everyone's pretty familiar with the statistics that people always like to float out about how many restaurants fail. There are a lot of things that go into making a restaurant successful — the right market, the right product, the right demographic, the right management, the right pricing, the right rent. There are a lot of things that go into it. The problem is often exactly what I said before – a lot of people try it with a misconception of what it takes to do it and what the job is going to be like. I think there's a lot of things they don't know. But, the one thing that I would suggest to anyone, and I know it may not sound like fun, but I always tell people if you want to open a restaurant the first thing you should do is work in a restaurant. That's the first thing you should do. It could be as a host, a busser, a waiter, a bartender, or a manager. Anything is better than nothing. Go and see how restaurants work and see what goes into the success. See how the margins are managed, etc., etc. I think you have to work in one in order to open one.

Parting thoughts?

If I could give people advice it would be that it seems a lot scarier than it is. And it's a risk. But a lot of things come with risk. This is something that people are really passionate about. I love the mom-and-pop restaurants. I love independents. Corporations are great too, but what really makes this industry special in my opinion is the individual owners. It's getting harder for people like that to operate. But it is possible. And I do believe the industry will see it through. I believe people have a lot of fortitude. To me, nothing will ever replace that independent restaurant that really nails it as far as an experience for people going out and having hospitality and dinner and celebrating things together. If you really love those sort of things it can make it all worth it. There are a lot of things that are scary and that are challenges. But the one thing I'll say to people is, "It's possible. You can do it. Get in there and work. Learn as much as you can." If you find the right opportunity, it really can work. A lot of those statistics of the failures include people that have never worked in the restaurant industry before and maybe have no idea what they're doing. If you have and you feel like you have a good idea of what you're doing and it's something that people want to do, I say go for it. Follow the right advice and take the right precautions, but this is a great industry and it can use more creative, genuinely hospitable people to open more places. I really believe that.

Marilyn Schlossbach

The Marilyn Schlossbach Group

SIX LOCATIONS ACROSS FIVE CONCEPTS - ASBURY PARK, NJ

RESTAURANT OWNER SINCE 1992

Tell me about your background and what got you into the restaurant business in the first place.

About thirty years ago my mother was diagnosed with terminal cancer. She had about a month to live. My brother was into macro-biotic foods and he decided to bring her up to a hospital in Massachusetts run by the Kushi Foundation to get her on a macro-biotic diet to see if that could help with what she was going through. And it did. I was eighteen years old at the time and I saw a person that I loved go from thirty days to live to a full remission. It was a partnership between her chemotherapy and her diet. As a young kid in the eighties, I surely grew up with a lot of processed junk food. That was the beginning of cheeses with color and junk food and diet sodas and all these things that were filled with things that you can't even pronounce. With my mother's clean food alteration, she was able to heal herself. That was an amazing transformation for me into the world of local foods and how they can not only fill your body and your stomach but they can fill your soul.

Also, my dad was much older. He was born in 1898 and he was sixty-five when I was born. When the trends of modern day food came into play in the late seventies/early eighties, my father was adamantly against all of that. He would say, "What do you need that for? You should just eat the plant. You should just eat the food. You don't need to add all that crap to it." Even with medicine. "What do you need to take all those pills for? Just go out and pick some mint and put it in tea. Or have some ginger." In his generation, that's what you did. You didn't have all these antibiotics and all these concoctions. Your food was what you grew or what you got from your neighbor who grew it and sold it. So, we are getting back to our roots, and that's a great place to be. Not to be righteous here though, I'm known to break open a bag of Doritos every once in a while, or have a pepperoni pizza. But day-to-day, it's not just about the food you consume, it's also about supporting your environment and your neighbor on that centrical process of sustainability that comes from growing food.

So, this was a foundation for me and I embarked on a little bit of a culinary journey. We had a chef at a restaurant that my brother owned at the time called Ocean, which was a French-Japanese sushi bar in Avalon, New Jersey, and I was a waitress. One weekend my brother was away and the chef didn't show up for some personal reasons and I went into the kitchen and got on the line and through my big portable phone with my brother and was able to be talked through an evening of craziness. The end result of it was that I was hooked. I felt the best I had ever felt in life about passion and my creative self. I come from a family of very adventurous people — artists and dancers and singers, explorers — and I never really had a talent that I innately could do for myself to make me passionate about the world. When I got on that line, something clicked. From that day forward that's what I did. I read every cookbook I could find. We didn't have the internet so we couldn't Google anything. You had to get all your resources from books and libraries. To this day, I have a cookbook collection of thousands of cookbooks that over the years have helped transform my culinary career and also inspired me in my travels and where I go and eat. I'm always looking for inspiration. But it all stems from a healing place for me as a woman, as a child, as a culinary inspiration.

After that night, you knew this is what you wanted to pursue?

I always knew what food was supposed to look like in the restaurant, and what customers' feedback on it was. But at that moment in time I had never prepped anything or cooked anything in that restaurant. So just knowing when to flip a piece of fish or steak over, I had to be talked through on the phone that night. There's just something about the restaurant industry that's *hypnotic and addictive*. It's very high paced and chaotic. I was used to those things because I did work on the floor and I loved the fast pace of the industry and the people. But when I got into the culinary world, for me it was a passion for food and the palate that I've been told I have a talent for. That is one of the innate things that a great chef has that you can't really be taught.

I was able to really hone into something special for myself that could please people, that was creative, but wasn't a traditional creative thing at that time, especially for women. Chefs weren't thought of as these great Hollywood stars that they are now. I was probably one of the only women in the industry that I knew, and definitely in the Japanese world. There were a lot of challenges, as a woman, with trying to deal with Japanese purveyors and chefs, but I didn't think of it that way. I just was really excited to have something I was passionate about. I was reading a great book called *Think and Grow Rich* that was written at the time of Andrew Carnegie, that talks about all these things that people who do great things have. One of them is *desire*, and one of them is *persistence*. You don't just think about it, you just do it.

When did you decide to open your own restaurant?

After that summer, I was driving south through a little town called Bayhead, New Jersey. It's a little coastal, sleepy winter town, but in the summer it's pretty vibrant. I saw a for rent sign on this cute little cottage, tucked back

194

behind this real estate office, down an alleyway. The whole alley was filled with edible flowers, and there was a cute courtyard with a beautiful garden and a little tiny house. I knocked on the door and asked the guy what was going on. He said the chef that was supposed to come in and have this restaurant backed out at the very last minute, and said he would give it to me for the season for three thousand dollars. In today's world, that doesn't seem like much for rent. But back then, I was twenty-one or twenty-two years old, I had just lost my parents, and I didn't have any money. I really wanted this so I got every friend I could to help me come up with the money and paint the place and decorate. I had all my cookbooks and I figured out a menu from all the dishes in the cookbooks that I liked.

I opened a restaurant called Rosalie's Kitchen. I named it after a woman who was the cleaning lady for Mark, a former boyfriend. She was an African-American woman from North Carolina. She was a beautiful soul and anytime I would be sick and I would be over at Mark's house, she would whip me up something from her garden, some sort of concoction with lemon grass or lemon balm or ginger. Back then that wasn't the norm in our world. In today's world everybody's very interested in farm-to-table and all different experiments with herbs and different vegetables and fruits. But back then, that was very rare. She was such an inspiration to me. We used to sit around and have tea and I would say, "Rosalie, if I ever have a restaurant someday, I'm going to name it after you because you are just a beautiful woman."

She was ninety-two when I opened the restaurant. I called Mark and I said, "You need to pass this message onto Rosalie that I finally opened my own restaurant and I named it after her." They brought her up from North Carolina that summer. I gave her a Rosalie's Kitchen T-shirt and she sat and had dinner with her little T-shirt on and she was so excited. It broke my heart that this woman wasn't going to be around much longer at that point. But I was so excited that she got to see Rosalie's Kitchen before she died.

That was the birth of my career, that little restaurant. It literally took me a whole season before I made a dish on that menu that wasn't out of a cookbook, but when it happened, all of my friends and family were so excited. I got a great review in the local paper and that was the birth of my career.

How long did you have Rosalie's?

I was there for five years. I met a guy — always about a guy — who convinced me to open another restaurant in Belmar called The Labrador Lounge. I have a Labrador Lounge now, but not the same location and not with him. Through a not-great relationship with a not-great human being, I went through a tough process and lost both of those restaurants — one forcibly by him and the other one because of him. I opened another small restaurant, but I hadn't healed as a person or as a chef, and that one failed. I went off the grid and became a snowboard rep and worked in the surf and snowboard industry for a while.

One of my customers saw me at a snowboard shop and was like, "What are you doing?" I said, "I had to get out of the business." That relationship really had done number on me mentally, financially and physically. It was a horrible couple of years. My customer had a bar in Mantoloking called Used to Be's. He said, "Well, I've got a kitchen and we never have good food here. How about if I just give you my kitchen and you cook great food. You can keep all the money you make in the kitchen. You don't have to pay me any rent. It would be a shame to see you get out of it because your food is so great." I was like, "Oh, I don't know." And he said, "Just try it for one summer and see if you like it." I said, "Okay, as long as we don't tell anybody. I don't want anybody knowing that I'm getting back into it. I just want to cook and see how I feel about it."

So I went in there and opened this little place called Café La Playa. Playa means "beach" in Spanish. I had a dog at the time, which, for some reason, responded to Spanish words. I don't know who taught her. But when you would say "Do you want to go to la playa?" she would freak out. If you'd say, "You want to go to the beach?" she didn't have any idea what you were talking about. So we named the restaurant after that little anecdote. And I cooked there for a few years. I had a great time. It was a bar-bar, it wasn't a restaurant bar. It was this wild, crazy summer bar. I had a blast. I got to make great food, and nobody knew that I was there. Then one day a local newspaper reporter brought one of the people from James Beard in there for dinner. I was so horrified, because this place was a drunk, down and dirty bar. This wasn't a place that somebody from James Beard Foundation came to eat. They ate and she called me and she said, "Minus all the drunks, it was an amazing meal."

She wrote a review about it and it gave me faith in my food again. It got me back on track to want to do a restaurant again — a real restaurant, not a loud crazy bar restaurant. My boyfriend and I were about to get engaged.

We ended up buying a building in Normandy Beach and I had the old Labrador sign in my garage. So we brought the Labrador Lounge back to life with a more positive relationship and a more positive situation. The guy who owned the building ended up financing it for us because we had no money, and his wife looked exactly like my mother. We all met, we bonded and I cried and it was just a wonderful experience. So, my culinary world has not made me the most money, but it has given me so many precious experiences with so many people that it's priceless.

What did you learn from the issues with Rosalie's and Labrador that benefited you as you got back into the business?

Relationships are key. The hospitality industry is *built around people and relationships*. It's a people-driven business, and it's an expensive business to be in when you need so many people involved in the process. It's complicated to deal with different temperaments and different ways of communication. Everybody comes from a different background with a different way of communicating with people. That is the most tiring thing about it. But in all of the restaurants I've had, there have been handfuls of people who are just really special people that I've gotten to know and be close with. Everyone teaches me something new about food and teaches me something new about being a business owner. I am self-taught. Everything I've learned mostly comes from mistakes I've made, honestly. And I've made more mistakes, probably, than most people because I've attempted to do more things than most people. But as I've grown and matured as a person and a business owner, the culinary for me now is less of the focus. It's more about learning about how to run a business, how to empower people in my business, and how to grow them as leaders so we can grow our company and open more businesses.

Now we're getting into other things like a cookbook and a food product and a toy product. We just launched Community Vine, a wine project, for our local foodbank. We're partnering with a wine maker and a distributor and raising money for food organizations. My focus is definitely not in the kitchen on the line anymore. But, I'm growing. I'm learning about all the things I have to do in the business, and some of them are not as pleasant as others, like the financials and the taxes and the payroll and all of that. But I've learned to make that rewarding by learning about it and trying to do it better every day. One of the great things about our businesses is that every day is an absolutely new day. *It's like an ocean. It's never the same, and people are never the same*. The moods are always different, the customers are always different. It's always challenging, but rewarding and interesting at the same time.

What are some of the more memorable mistakes you've made along the way that you've learned from?

Most of my mistakes were either with individual employees that I didn't know how to communicate with well in order to get both of us to perform better as people, or financial mistakes. When I was young, I made a lot of financial mistakes — I owed people money, I didn't pay taxes the right way. I had a very brief restaurant that was in-between the bad relationships and the Labrador and then my break into the snowboard world, called the Karma Café. It was only open for a brief period of time because I was really damaged as a person and I just couldn't make the right choices in life. I needed to heal but I was young and I thought I could handle anything and I didn't feel that this person had hurt me as bad as he did. I owed a lot of people money when that restaurant closed. It took me a few years to pay people off and to write letters to people. One of them I wrote a letter to and I sent the check for around three thousand dollars for a plumbing bill that I never paid. I'm still paying off some of that restaurant to this day. I vowed that I would pay everybody back. I sent him a check and a letter explaining where I was at and why it took so long and my fear of contacting him. He wrote me back with the voided check and said, "You know, I've been following you and I see all the great things that you've done for people and I know how hard all of that was for you. I can't take your money. I'll always support you." That meant a lot because that was a really tough time to overcome. For a person like me, when you don't pay your debt in life it carries a lot of guilt. That response was really special, a memory I'll always have.

Our business in general is a business of passion. If you're in this business, it's not just for the money. It's not the biggest motivating factor and the margins are not that great for hospitality on an a la carte restaurant level. Because we're very driven as people in this industry by our creativity and our passion, it's very easy to get sucked into a building or a space because of what it looks like or where it is or a memory that you had. I've done it. I had a beautiful, wonderful restaurant that everybody loved called Trinity and the Pope. It was inspired by a trip to New Orleans. The building looked like it could have been on any street in New Orleans. We fell in love with it and we created this great restaurant. We had *New York Times* articles. It was wonderful. But it was in a really bad location. It was on a one-way street going the wrong way. No parking. No one could find us. I sometimes drove home from my other restaurant down the street, and because it was one-way and the wrong direction, I would drive right by and not even check on it — that's how much I didn't think about it because of where it was. What I learned from that is that you've got to do your homework when you get into a lease or into a restaurant situation. You have to do it for *financial reasons as well as passion*. At the end of the day, a dollar's a dollar, and if you overspend it those dollars add up and someday you're going to up and not be able to pay your bills.

I just had a call the other day about somebody wanting to come to Asbury Park. I said, "You've got to do your homework here. You've got to come in the winter, you've got to come during the week, you've got to look at the demographics. You can't just come here in the summer when it's fun and vibrant and there are tons of people everywhere, and say you're going to create a successful business here." We're very seasonal where we live. Even though people live here year-round, their patterns in the winter are very different than they are in the summer. We'll hibernate more, and they have kids in school functions and they don't go out all the time. People come in the restaurants on Saturday night and in the summer, and they're like, "Gosh, you make a lot of money. Look at this place. It's packed." I'm like, "Well, try it today — Monday, raining, Jersey Shore. I probably have two tables."

That's a big one — doing your homework, reaching out to people that you feel confidant to give you advice on the situation. Negotiating a lease is an arduous process. I'm in one right now. I was in one for a project for a year-and-a-half, and then we didn't do the project, because it just didn't make sense at the end of the day. We couldn't get the number to where both sides could be happy. We had to walk away from all that work and money that we had put into it. But if I did it, I'd probably not be there long enough to reap any rewards.

Having the discipline to walk away, despite how great the location seems, is important.

With Trinity I could have gone to New Orleans like a dozen times, stayed in the finest places and eaten in the finest restaurants for the amount of money we lost. Sometimes it just doesn't make sense. And that's hard.

How have you evolved as a manager during your years in the business?

Authentic communication is probably the key to life. If I had to give advice, it would be communication is what you should be confidently working on doing better. That is probably the toughest thing for people to do because everybody communicates differently. We've all been raised differently. We've heard different things programed into our brain as a kid.

We lived in different circumstances. It's by far the hardest thing to maneuver, but the most important challenge to overcome with people. I'm good at it when I put my mind to it, but it's one of the hardest things for me to take on with people. You can tell people exactly how you feel but sometimes people don't hear what you're saying, and you have to figure out how to say it to them in a way that they can hear. That is an ongoing process for me in leadership — how to be able to talk to people so you're not hurtful and you're not mean, but you're also making them understand the situation the way you want them to. It's tough. When I can master that I will be a great leader.

When you started there weren't a lot of female chefs and women restaurant owners. How has that changed over the years?

There are a lot more women getting into the industry, which is wonderful. When I started I was shocked to see that that wasn't the case because as a kid, I thought women were what food was. My mother cooked. My aunts cooked. I had no idea that in the food world, it was a very conservative mentality, and a male-dominated industry. Me being a liberal woman was a rarity. Over time, I think that's shifted. I think all the food shows have been very beneficial in opening up the doors to all kinds of people to be in the industry. With that comes some obstacles because a lot of people going into the industry think this is like a movie set and you're going to be a rock star because you're a chef. *It's hard work*. Being in a hot kitchen, producing great food — producing any kind of food, honestly — is not the most glamorous position to be in. It's not TV. You're not walking around in perfect clothing and air conditioning, making little perfect dishes. You're working hard with a whole team that you have to maneuver in and get them motivated to do things in a very orchestrated way. It's very high-pace in a very hot space.

I speak at culinary schools and sit on advisory boards, and it's a lot of money to go to culinary school. They think, "Oh, I cook at home. I love entertaining." Then they go to culinary school and get a job in a restaurant and they're like, "Whoa, this isn't what I do." Personally, I never get to enjoy an all-day cooking experience with nice music and air conditioning — that just doesn't happen in our world. And people have to realize that. I always say to people who come to me and say they want to go to culinary school, "Start by working in a kitchen first. See if you can handle it. Because it's not always pleasant. And you have to be prepared for that." The dichotomy of going out into the dining room and seeing all these people having fun and it's air conditioned and they're having cocktails, and then you're in the back, sweating, and everybody's yelling to pick up this and do this and flip this — it's very different. I love it. There's nothing more beautiful to me than a kitchen that is working in harmony. ***It's like a beautiful orchestra***. But it doesn't always happen. There's a lot of players and a lot of temperaments in that, and they're all working long hours in very hot space, which can be aggravating. I love that it has expanded, but I also want there to be a balance of reality for people getting into this business. It's not all show here.

What else do you love about this industry?

The lives you can change through what you do. We've had so many different types of people work for us and when you are able to lift them up and change them and get them passionate about what you're doing, that is when you have success. That is a great feeling as a business owner to be able to do that. And for sure, there's a hundred people for every one you lift up that you can't get to buy into your Kool-Aid. But, you have to relish the one that you do, because if you can replicate that in some way you're going to change lives. And that happens with your customers too, with the way you nourish them.

Give me a summary of where you are with your group of businesses and projects.

We have five restaurants. We just bought a new one beginning of the summer in a more year-round location. We're trying to balance out our seasonality a little bit. The wine, called Community Vines, came out last week. We have a ketchup we're working on called Kula Ketchup, which will be a community project for the Kula Café, a non-profit café that I began in Asbury Park. We have a toy template in production right now called Libby the Lobster. It's a toddler toy that we're going to use to raise money for environmental catastrophes like Sandy, to help small businesses and small communities recover. The cookbook is eleven chapters for eleven charities. It's a charity-based cookbook and it's beautiful – three hundred and twenty pages of gorgeous photography and recipes compiled with many friends and chefs over the years. We're also working on a salt that we've been making in-house but we're not that far along with that yet. We've got a bunch of stuff in the works. We're always looking to grow, but we're trying to do it in different areas now, not necessarily all in a la carte dining. This helps us balance finances for our employees and ourselves. But we always have something brewing.

We're doing a food truck, too. It's called The Ohana Kitchen and Farm Stand. It's a non-profit. We have a non-profit called Food for Thought by the Sea. We've been fundraising for this truck and we have some grant applications in. It's going to be a community truck, no community left behind, and we're partnering with other non-profits to raise money for them and bring awareness to their causes by moving this feast around our community. That is probably the biggest thing we'll be working on in the next year.

Any last words of wisdom?

I just think anybody who has a passion should just go for it. *Life should be filled with passion.*

ACKNOWLEDGEMENTS

This book would never have happened if the amazing owners we featured weren't so generous with their time. Like all restaurant owners, they are very busy and are often juggling tons of things at once. All of us here at Schedulefly offer our sincere thanks to Rayme, Steve, Bret, Meherwan, Rob, Paul, Jess, Kimberly, Cris, Angela, Seth, Scott, Van, Travis, Lisa, Sean D., Shawn, Sean S., Kiersten, Keith, and Marilyn. We admire you and respect you, and we are super-proud to serve you and your teams with our software.

Rita Hedden works at Word Processing Pros. You can find them at www.wordprocessingpros.com. She transcribed all of the interviews. You can automate the transcription process but I don't trust it and I much prefer to work with people. Rita is awesome. She's reliable, quick and accurate.

Melanie Strain is a former colleague at a previous business. I have tons of respect for her and feel lucky that she was willing to help with this book. She took all of the raw transcriptions and cut out my rambling questions and made the content clean and crisp. That's a very critical part of the process, and I owe her a gigantic thank you!

Luke Pearson has designed the book cover for both of our books. He also produces all of the videos in our People of Indie Restaurants video series. He's a highly talented dude and you can find him at www.liftfilms.net.

We don't know who the 15,000 or so people who have bought our first Restaurant Owners Uncorked book are, but we appreciate them and they should know that they are a big part of the reason this book exists. When we published that book five years ago, we had no clue what would happen. I was worried we would sell less than twenty copies, mostly to friends and family. But we sold several hundred copies the first month, and hundreds the next month, and it has sold well ever since. So if you bought it, thank you. We truly mean that. And we hope you got something out of it.

Wes, Tyler, Charles and Hank are my business partners. They support me working on incredible projects like our books, podcasts, and videos, and I am grateful for that. Your support means the stories of many incredible restaurant owners are being told. Thank you.

OTHER RESTAURANT OWNERS UNCORKED PROJECTS

Book: *Restaurant Owners Uncorked: Twenty Owners Share Their Recipes for Success* available on Amazon.

Podcast: Restaurant Owners Uncorked, available on iTunes. Every owner featured in this book is on our podcast, as well as many others.

Videos: Restaurant Owners Uncorked video series, available on Vimeo. Several of the owners featured in this book are featured in our video series, as well as many others.

ABOUT THE AUTHOR

WIL BRAWLEY

I'm one of the five guys at Schedulefly, a North Carolina-based restaurant employee scheduling software company started in 2007. We published our first book, *Restaurant Owners Uncorked: Twenty Owners Share Their Recipes for Success* in 2011, and we produce the Restaurant Owners Uncorked podcast series on iTunes and Restaurant Owners Uncorked video series on Vimeo. Check 'em out! We're going to keep sharing restaurant owners' stories as long as we are able. I'm at wbrawley@schedulefly.com if you'd ever like to touch base.

Printed in Great Britain
by Amazon

34022335R00122